Seldom will you have heard the \
book. It's written with an artistr
passion directed to lead you to pı
her recovery of Scripture's unity, c

life-changing power. This work satisfies the reader on so many levels at once: straightforward Bible study, warm pastoral proclamation, careful cultural assessment, and a taste of rejoicing that only God's children know. What a gift for storytelling! What a pleasure to read! More, more, I say!

Nelson D. Kloosterman, Professor of New Testament and Ethics, Mid-America Reformed Seminary

For many the Old Testament is only a collection of stories about ancient individuals. What is lacking is the grand redemptive thread that ties those stories together in Christ. This book traces that thread through the feasts that shaped Israel's annual calendar, anticipated Jesus' coming, and defined his gospel. It will change the way you read the Bible. I strongly recommend this book for use by individuals, Sunday school classes, and small groups.

Dr. Charles Dunahoo, Director of Christian Education and Publications, Presbyterian Church in America

Many see the name Jesus and immediately think of the New Testament, but his presence is the scarlet thread running through the pages of the Old Testament as well. In *Meeting Jesus at the Feast,* John Sittema pulls back the curtain on the Hebrew festivals of the Old Testament to reveal Jesus sitting at the head of the table. He brings to light how each of the God-ordained feasts and festivals point to a future manifestation of the person and work of Jesus Christ. By unveiling the purpose and passion behind each of the seven celebrations, John helps us grasp a deeper and richer understanding of God's redemptive plan through his Son.

Sharon Jaynes, Author of *Building an Effective Women's Ministry* and *The Power of a Woman's Words*

Sittema's book presents in a fresh way the story of God's coming to us in Jesus Christ to mend the brokenness of human life under the power of sin. Jesus Christ fulfills all the biblical promises of shalom that God's renewed people and world already experience in this life, but not fully as in the life to come. Throughout his stimulating study, Sittema artfully weaves together the biblical story of redemption through Jesus Christ with the stories of believers who are experiencing the transforming power of the gospel.

Dr. Cornel Venema, President, Mid-America Reformed Seminary and author of *Christ and the Future: The Bible's Teaching on the Last Things*

Clear and precise, *Meeting Jesus* is an insightful study into the festivals God himself instituted among His chosen people. Their universal significance and ultimate meaning would be revealed by the life, death, and resurrection of his Son, Jesus Christ, bearing tremendous consequences for all of mankind. An essential read for new and long-time Christians alike for a deeper understanding and appreciation of our hopeless past, redeemed present, and the glorious future that awaits us.

"B," leader in the Chinese house church movement (name withheld by request)

This book is filled with breathtaking insights into the Scriptures. These become sweet moments in which you will see the greatness of Jesus Christ as he is revealed in both the Old and New Testament Scriptures.

Frank Reich, M. Div., President of Reformed Theological Seminary and pastor, former NFL quarterback

Meeting JESUS AT THE FEAST:

Israel's Festivals and the Gospel

JOHN R. SITTEMA

Reformed Fellowship, Inc.
3500 Danube Dr. SE,
Grandville, MI 49418

Reformed Fellowship, Inc., is a religious and strictly nonprofit organization composed of a group of Christian believers who hold to the biblical Reformed faith. Its purpose is to advocate and propagate this faith, to nurture those who seek to live in obedience to it, to give sharpened expression to it, to stimulate the doctrinal sensitivities of those who profess it, to promote the spiritual welfare and purity of the Reformed churches, and to encourage Christian action.

Cover Design by Greg Ratzlaff
Interior design by Jeff Steenholdt & Erika De Vries

Printed in the United States of America

ISBN 978-1-935369-00-4

For my Mother, Jeanette Sittema,
who taught me the story
and showed me the thread

Contents

Introduction

Imagine . . . morning in New York on a late summer day. Your husband Kevin is ready to walk out the door to catch the train into Manhattan. Just before he does, you confront him about the light switch he promised to fix over the weekend but didn't. Again. You exchange cross words. He grabs his backpack and travel mug and storms out the door without giving you a kiss. You know you'll smooth things over that night when he gets home, but you already feel a ten-pound weight on your heart. Should you run after him? You decide not to. Two hours later, your neighbor bangs on the door, shouting at you to turn on the TV. When you do, your heart stops. A familiar reporter is making an announcement. His voice is agitated; he shuffles papers and fumbles for words. Images flash across the screen: one airplane . . . two airplanes . . . crashing into the Twin Towers of the World Trade Center. (Your mind is whirling. *This can't be real; it must be a movie.*) The massive towers explode, burn, and collapse in a fiery heap. But Kevin works there! The phone begins to ring. It won't stop for days.

Imagine . . . having cancer. You're worn out, weakened by chemotherapy and radiation, weary beyond description. You've been in treatment for years; it has become so much a part of your life that you can't remember not being sick. There are always tests: tests to see if your blood is back to normal, tests to find out if the treatment is effective, if another protocol will be necessary. At the beginning, the tests scared you; these days they just add to the weariness. A knock at the door. The whole medical team enters the room—that's a bad sign, isn't it?—but your doctor is smiling. He says simply, "Everything worked great. The cancer is gone! Go home and live a little. You deserve it!" You pack fast while your driver pulls the car around, repeatedly looking at the door, fearful that they made a mistake and will return to correct it. You leave the building stunned and just a bit numb, but by the time you arrive at home, the shock is over. You start making phone calls immediately. News this good simply must be shared. A party is on for that evening!

Powerful announcements like these—whether delivered in image form on TV or in person by a doctor—*look back* to something that has already happened and thus cause you to take stock, to reflect, to regret, to grieve, to celebrate. But they also *look forward* to an unknown future. Because of one simple announcement, life changes, and your mind races with the possibilities.

The gospel—literally "good news"—of Jesus Christ is an announcement that changed everything. I don't mean the kind of change where you commit to wearing your seatbelt regularly, squeeze another child's soccer schedule into an already too-full life, or cut carbs out of your diet. I mean change the way 9/11 changed U.S. history, the way being cleared of cancer changes a person's life. I mean breathtaking change—a 10 on the Richter scale change. Jesus' arrival on the world scene to a stable in Bethlehem did more than add a Hallmark moment to late December schedules; it announced the arrival of a king more majestic and powerful than Caesar himself, one who would make Caesar's Rome distant and ancient history. The reports of his simple life, cruel death, and covered-up resurrection made news so incredible that it impacts the future of every human who has ever lived or ever will live. Jesus the Messiah did not merely provide a good example or launch a religion; he changed the world.

A paragraph like the previous one, with assertions seemingly so over the top, simply begs the question. "Show me how," you may be thinking. "Tell me how this can be, how you know such a thing is true."

The Bible does just that. More than just a book of rules and regulations or a collection of character studies from which you can learn ethics or techniques for self-improvement, the Bible is a *story*, and a unique one at that. It is the story of God and the history of his redemption, a God who saves people, to be sure, but also one who restores the whole of the cosmos. Jesus is the key to the story, the main character, the central thread around which God weaves the astonishing tapestry of salvation.

That can be hard to understand. It can seem harder still to believe down deep. It takes the kind of faith only God can give. Do you know what was more difficult than believing what happened in the past? Believing that Jesus was the point of the story long *before* he arrived on the world scene. Yet that is just what God asked of the ancient people of Israel: to put their faith and hope in a Redeemer and Messiah who would not make his appearance for more than a thousand years.

To help his people see and identify the coming Messiah—although faintly, and still in the distant future—God made promises to the patriarchs Abraham, Isaac, and Jacob. He used Moses and the prophets to point Israel's gaze forward through the words of the Torah and the prophetic writings. One of the most significant ways he helped an ancient people to believe was by giving them a series of feasts or festivals that would shape both their daily life and their annual calendars. Each of these provided a hint, a clue, of the One who was coming. More than just information, each feast was a taste to whet their appetites and build anticipation and excitement.

God also wants people today, some two thousand years *after* Messiah's appearance, to know that Jesus—and particularly his cross and resurrection—did change everything, to believe and trust in him, and to follow him with a whole heart. But people today struggle with faith's claim just as those in ancient times struggled to believe the promises God gave them. Belief seems difficult when all you hear about Jesus is that he was a good man, was humble, taught well, and died a horrible death. Those factoids are only bits and bytes of data that are often unconnected to the story, but they are the only pieces of information that many will ever know about Jesus.

Sadly, data processing does not qualify as authentic and dynamic faith.

This book aims to tell you more about Jesus. Much more. By unpacking and explaining the ancient feasts, it aims to give modern people a fuller vision of the good news of God, reveal just what it means that Jesus is the Messiah, and explain how and why his coming changed the world.

For the feasts, commissioned twelve hundred years before Jesus came, were celebrations about him. First, they anticipated his coming. Then they *defined* his life and ministry. In fact, you cannot really comprehend what it means that Jesus is Messiah without knowing something about the feasts. All the significant moments in his ministry (both his earthly ministry and his ministry from heaven's throne after the ascension) were divinely structured around them. Consider:

- Jesus' death was pointedly timed to take place on *Passover.*
- Jesus' burial was specifically timed to occur on the *Feast of Unleavened Bread.*
- His resurrection waited for the dawning of *Firstfruits.*
- The outpouring of the Spirit came precisely fifty days later, on the *Feast of Pentecost.*
- The *Feast of Trumpets* defines the Spirit-filled church's task: to preach the gospel.
- The *Day of Atonement* defines just what being saved really means.
- The *Feast of Tabernacles* shows what it is to live in the joy of fellowship with Christ.
- And *Jubilee* teaches us what heaven is and will be like, tilting us forward to its glory, grace, and final rest.

If Jesus' entire ministry was structured around the feasts, it seems important for us to understand why. Turn the page and join me as we meet Jesus at the feast!

FROM RESTLESSNESS TO REST— SABBATH AS THE MOVEMENT OF HISTORY

Old Testament		*New Testament*
Creation	**Fall**	**Redemption**
Rest as Delight	*Restlessness in Sin*	*Rest Restored*
Sabbath as Shalom (Gen 2:2–3)	Sabbath as Longing *Rest Remembered* *(Ex 20:8)* *Rest Anticipated* *(Isa 61)*	Sabbath in Christ *Jubilee Inaugurated* *(Already) (Lk 4)* *Jubilee Consummated* *(not yet) (Rev 22)*

Diagram 1.1: Sabbath as the Movement of History

Chapter 1

Rehearsing Rest

The Sabbaths

Leviticus 23:1–3

A few years ago, a Christian friend who is a film producer shared an insight with me that changed the way I watch movies. He observed that most good stories—those that resonate with an audience—seem to have similar plot elements. They open by portraying life lived in happiness and joy. All is well. Conflict soon intrudes, though, in the form of changing circumstances or with the arrival of a new character, and the result disrupts life and brings a dissonance you can feel in your gut. Key to the story is how the conflict is resolved: redemption comes, usually at great personal cost, and it is this cost that is the heart of the story. It is this cost that connects with the viewer.[1]

I've watched films through that lens ever since. I'd bet my friend's observations are true for your favorite films as they are for mine. I have always been a Tolkien fan (my wife would use a stronger word), and although Peter Jackson's films do not do justice to Tolkien's books, the Lord of the Rings trilogy is wonderful, bigger than life in its scope, and complex in its plot, language, and characterization. What makes it so compelling is that it is a story of redemption that comes at a shockingly great cost; it is that cost that makes the end so satisfying.

1 I am indebted to Gregg Easterbrook for this insight.

Of course, redemption stories are not the only popular genre. Quite different is the genre of tragedy, a form of literature, theater, or film as old as the Greeks. In tragedies, it is not redemption, but the misery of a sinful or broken world that is under close view. In tragedies, the chief character typically meets a disastrous fate, the broader ills of society often exposed in the tale. I recently viewed *No Country for Old Men,* the Coen brothers' film based on Cormac McCarthy's novel. There is barely time after the opening credits to start the camera before gut-wrenching violence fills the screen. Senseless brutality dominates the film to the end. All the good people die, while the wretched murderer survives to destroy another day. The lives of simple people in rural West Texas are depicted as meaningless activity as they scurry about like ants struggling for survival, but all the while their lives are actually controlled by a cruel chance. It alone drives their fate; the flip of a coin—several times—is the sole determiner of life or death. Redemption? None comes. The film leaves viewers devoid of hope as the screen snaps black. Everyone in the theater in which I viewed the film sat in stunned silence for several minutes after the film ended, refusing to believe it had ended as it did.

While tragedies have always been an important literary genre, they *feel* less satisfying because they tell an unfinished truth. Ugliness and evil abound in the real world, to be sure, and their power is horrid. No one is exempt from their reach; good people feel the pain as much as the bad guys. But our souls desperately want to believe that there is more to life than tragedy.

Redemptive themes satisfy us more deeply, not only because we prefer to feel good when we leave a theater, but, suggested my friend, because such movies reflect the fuller truth of God's story. God's story isn't stuck on the tragic; he pursues redemption relentlessly. The movement of redemption is not only nice, it is normative, shaping our understanding of life because it is the movement of life.

The Plot

On my mother's knee, I memorized a rhyme that would serve me well as a guide whenever I picked up the Bible. To explain the plot of redemption running through the Bible's two covenants, she taught me, "The New is in the Old concealed; the Old is by the New revealed." Behind this saying lay her conviction that the Bible is one story, its narrative like a golden thread that wound its way through the pages of history. The golden thread, of course, is the coming of Jesus the Christ.

The plot of the Bible is dramatic and is set forth in three acts: Creation—Fall—Redemption.[2] The first two acts are very short and, in fact, are presented in just a few pages in the Bible's first book, Genesis. But their brevity does not belie their significance: understanding creation and fall correctly is essential to a proper understanding of the rest of the Bible, the divine act of redemption.

Creation

In the opening chapter of the Bible, we read that God "created the heavens and the earth." No mere polemic against evolution—Darwin was, after all, a long ways off—the issue in the opening words of the Bible is not whether or even when God created the heavens and the earth, but who he is and what the world is in relation to him. God is Creator, and creation—"the heavens and the earth" together in harmonious unity—is presented as his domain, his kingdom, and he its sovereign king.

Under his rule, creation has a dynamic character: God assigned active dominion responsibility to the sun (the greater light) "to govern the day" and to the moon (the lesser light) "to govern the night" skies. He established limits for the reproductive processes in the plant and animal kingdoms ("according to their kinds"). God, the greater King, also gave dominion responsibility to Adam, the lesser king, mandating him to subdue the earth and to rule over everything (Genesis 1:28).

Adam was not granted divine permission to do what he wanted with creation; he was to exercise responsible dominion, always under God, the Sovereign (Genesis 1:26–28). Under his care, creation was to bring praise to God in new ways. Adam's *identity* was that of image-bearer of God; his work would also image God's. As God had "separated" light from dark, atmosphere from planet surface, and land from sea, so Adam's cultural mandate called him and his seed to separate—to differentiate and develop—the creation entrusted to him. Minerals gathered from the ground would be studied, understood, and combined to produce pigments that would one day, in the hands of Da Vinci,

2 Craig G. Bartholomew and Michael W. Goheen further divide redemption into initiation (Old Testament Israel), accomplishment (Christ's earthly ministry and that of the missionary church), and completion (Christ's return). *The Drama of Scripture: Finding Our Place in the Biblical Story* (Grand Rapids, Michigan: Baker Academic, 2004). Christopher J. H. Wright, in *The Mission of God: Unlocking the Bible's Grand Narrative* (Downer's Grove: IVP Academic, 2006), sees the history of redemption as missiological, both of God and for his people.

create the *Mona Lisa* (and in mine, paint the garage). Antonio Vivaldi, in hearing, capturing, and reproducing the sounds of the wind and the rain in the changing seasons of the weather, would ultimately give us another kind of *Four Seasons* with which to praise God.

Creation, when God finished it, was perfect. When he surveyed his realm, he spoke with royal voice: "It is very good!" He *rested* the seventh day (Genesis 2:2–3). He wasn't tired; Sabbath makes its first appearance in the biblical narrative to mark God's joy, his celebration and delight that creation was just the way it was supposed to be. The Bible would later call such harmony *shalom*.

But the joy was short lived. Sin slithered in through a rebel who challenged the authority of the King of creation by inciting doubt in his royal word ("Did God really say . . . ?"). Corrupting everything God made with horrible effectiveness, sin warped all that had been very good so that it is now "not the way it's supposed to be."[3] Theologians call this the fall, but the word hardly does justice to the devastation. A marriage that had begun with a "Wow!" became cloaked in a clumsy leaf-shroud of shame, while a delightful evening garden walk between God and his right-hand man morphed into a guilty game of hide and seek. In a rapid-fire series of judicial pronouncements, God cursed Satan, sentenced Adam, and then his wife. The woman, created to rest in the tender love of a husband and rejoice in the life-affirming gift of birth, would instead groan in labor and chafe under his dominance. The man, created to be happy and productive in his labor and to rest in the sweet weariness that comes at the end of a long day of work, would now taste the bitterness and frustration of toil. God's gleeful delight in a colorful creation that was deemed "very good" gave way to a bleak wasteland of human hopelessness, rendered now only in shades of gray.

Redemption

But wait! Peeking up from the rubble of a world gone bad, a fragile light flickered, all the more noticeable because of the strange timing of its appearance. God simply couldn't wait to redeem; his promise of redemption was spoken in the same breath as his curse, the flame of hope lit even before the pronouncement of sentence. Juxtaposing hope over against the cold horror of long warfare, the Royal One declared his intent: he will crush Satan; he will win victory through the "seed of the woman."

---

3 Cornelius Plantinga, *Not the Way It's Supposed to Be: A Breviary of Sin* (Grand Rapids, Michigan: Eerdman's Publishing Company, 1996).

God will make right all that sin has made wrong. God will restore shalom and give his people rest again. Because of sin, creation had become—and still is—restless. Once thrilled that his creation was "very good," God no longer delights in what is; he, and all creation with him, yearn now for what should be, for what will be.

Restoring joy and bringing rest would involve conflict. In Genesis 3:15, God had promised Satan "enmity between you and the woman." The long war would be for man's benefit: we must know the cost of our sin and learn in faith to long for God's redemption. But the outcome was never in question. God assured that he would triumph through "the seed of the woman." His promise would allow the fragile candle of hope to flicker, despite the winds of war in a world that would witness fratricide (4:8), terrorist threats (4:23–24), and ethical anarchy: "every inclination of the thoughts of [man's] heart was only evil all the time" (6:5).

Rehearsals, Types, and Shadows

Once, when my children were small, we vacationed near the Pea Ridge Civil War battlefield in northwest Arkansas. The day was beautiful and the site well preserved. I was not prepared for the frustration we would experience for a full morning. Simply put, we had no clue what we were viewing. The park was enormous, and without a map that showed us what the key locations were and how the battle had progressed, we would remain frustrated.

On the way toward God's rest, his people needed help too. Struggling each day with the tension of enmity, they would easily lose the big-picture perspective of faith. Through the centuries, God sometimes intervened directly with his mighty hand to stimulate their faith, acting in ways both mighty and tender: crushing a mighty foe here, opening a closed womb there. But he also worked in ways more subtle. To shape the daily routines of the people of Israel, a people whose history began well over a thousand years before Messiah and whose faith would therefore need serious staying power, he established festivals that would both structure life and serve as portraits of redemption. These festivals are prescribed in Leviticus 23 and reveal from varying angles the wonder and grace of his redeeming work.

God called his festivals "appointed feasts" and "sacred assemblies" (Leviticus 23:1–2). Several Hebrew words lay behind these English translations. The first of these—the Hebrew word *mo'ed*—defines all the festivals as "set feasts" established by the LORD and regulated by his commands. Among these set feasts were the *haggim*, three pilgrimage festivals requiring Israel to travel annually to a central location. The name is appropriate; the singular *hag* evokes movement and suggests a joyous dance.

In the book of Leviticus, another term nuanced all the festivals. The term *miqra qodesh*—usually translated "sacred assemblies"—suggests a convocation that had a religious purpose, one shaped by hope.[4] To Israel, camped at Sinai at the dawn of her life as a redeemed people, God's sacred assemblies were not established merely to commemorate past acts of redemption but also to serve as "rehearsals" of what was to come.[5] When Israel was summoned to one of the pilgrimage festivals or when her families gathered in homes or village streets to celebrate the others, her eye—and her faith—were to be fixed on the future. Israel was not like the nations around her whose cultic gatherings were attempts to pacify the demands of pagan gods, angry for last year's failures, in a desperate form of bargaining for next year's blessings on crop and womb. Israel's feasts would not require her to barter with God. They were established after she had been delivered from bondage in Egypt, already freed by God's amazing grace, redeemed by that grace to be his special people. The feasts were designed to lean forward, to give life a future tilt, pointing her relentlessly to the Messiah who would fulfill all that the feasts portrayed.

Each festival was a type of Messiah. Derived from the Greek word *tupos, type* is commonly understood to refer to the use of the Old Testament to provide models, human figures whose lives serve as examples of Christian virtues or character traits. Thus, Daniel is said to be a type of Christian courage, David a type of godly friendship (Jonathan narratives) or of true repentance (Bathsheba narrative). The word *tupos* is even translated as "example" in most contemporary versions of 1 Corinthians 10:6.[6]

But such a use of *type* is thin. The word actually connotes something much richer, the notion of a foretaste, an advance presentation of the whole.[7] An example of tonight's dinner could be milk and cookies, arranged by

4 James Swanson, *Dictionary of Biblical Languages with Semantic Domains: Hebrew (Old Testament)*, electronic ed., s. v. "miqra," #5246.

5 James Strong, *The New Strong's Dictionary of Hebrew and Greek Words*, electronic ed., s. v. #4744.

6 Notably, the older RSV renders the word as "warnings."

7 *Tupos* serves as a technical term meaning precisely that. See Gerhard Kittel, *Theological Dictionary of the New Testament*, ed. G. Friedrich, vol. 8 (Grand Rapids, Michigan: Wm. B. Eerdmans Publishing Co., 1972), 251–2.

a four-year-old and presented with dramatic flair on downsized plastic dinnerware to a gathering of dolls seated neatly around a cardboard dining table. It is a play meal, different in substance from tonight's family dinner. Not so a *type.* Last Christmas, impatient for the holiday feast still fifteen minutes away, I sneaked into the kitchen like a cat burglar to pilfer a tasty morsel of the standing rib roast that would anchor our family meal. It had just been removed from the oven and was resting on a rack while the balance of the feast was being prepared. Knowing I'd be alone for just a few ticks of the clock, I activated both hands in my nefarious plot. With my right, I quickly sliced a not-too-thin corner of the succulent beef—redolent in spices, crusty with caramelized fat, and brimming with roasting juices—and with my left I soaked an end piece of crusty sourdough bread in the meat drippings just before using it as a scoop for garlic mashed potatoes—perfectly seasoned and steamy hot—which delivered to my nostrils and my mouth the beginnings of ecstasy. Rudely apprehended by the cook who shooed me irreverently out of the kitchen, I was shamefully unrepentant. I consumed the evidence slowly, like chewing cud, lost in the reverie and longing for more.

A children's play party may give an idea of food and drink. A type—like my samplings of the beef and potatoes—makes your mouth water because it is an early taste of the actual feast to come. That's how the ancient feasts of Israel served the people of God. More than religious play acting, they gave God's people a real and authentic taste of the redemption Messiah would bring centuries later, a taste that would make them long in faith and hope for the fuller revelation of the gift of God.

Speaking to a different culture a thousand years later, the apostle Paul used another metaphor to make the same point. He called the festivals "shadows" (Colossians 2:17). Think of a man walking westbound on a brilliant sunny morning. As the rising sun warms his back, his shadow stretches out before him, reaching the corner well before he does. His shadow is not merely an example of him but is inseparably connected to his very person. It announces that his arrival is at hand. More, his shadow provides many real and telling clues about him, clues like size and shape and the speed with which he walks. The clues may be indistinct, but since they are cast by a real person, they are authentic.

The story of the Bible is the story of Jesus the Messiah. He is the main character, the One who cast shadows as he moved relentlessly through history toward his incarnation in Bethlehem of Judea. That shadow appeared to ancient Israel in her sacrifices and festivals, each one awakening expectations about the promised Messiah and the redemption he would bring. Somewhat indistinct, not easily identified in a single glance, always requiring faith and constant explanation, his shadow was nonetheless the promise of him, a very real portrayal of "the reality" which "is found in Christ" (Colossians 2:17).

It's All about Rest

At the base of Sinai, God would give his people seven festivals that would function like individual frames in a reel of film, a series of feasts that would serve to give them glimpses of Messiah's shadow. There was an additional feast, however, one established at the same time and in the same biblical passage, that was distinct from the other seven and, in fact, framed all of them. Leviticus 23 begins with this feast, a celebration known as *Sabbath.* Its name suggests the idea of rest, and its commemoration would shade all the other feasts with a unique hue. Redemption in its rich and variegated dimensions—as seven festivals would soon show—was about the bringing of rest and the restoration of shalom. If the Bible is a story, its dramatic movement is from restlessness toward Sabbath rest.[8]

Sabbath was not only one day per week. Actually, there were Sabbaths (plural), as Israel was soon to learn, and they were to be commemorated every seventh day, every seventh year, and, in the year of Jubilee, the Sabbath of Sabbaths, a year-long celebration following the seventh cycle of seven years.

Keeping the Sabbaths involved first of all heeding the call to remember. But what was Israel to remember? In its first appearance in Scripture (Genesis 2), resting involved remembering creation. God himself rested and remembered with delight the work he had done in creating the heavens and the earth. Later, in the first giving of the Decalogue (Exodus 20:8–11), God grounded Israel's Sabbath-keeping in this creation rest: "Remember the Sabbath day by keeping it holy . . . For in six days the Lord made the heavens and the earth, the sea, and all that is in them, but he rested on the seventh day. Therefore the LORD blessed the Sabbath day and made it holy."

In calling Israel to remember, God wanted her to do more than recall Genesis 1 and the fact that he had made all things. God wanted her to grapple with the wondrous truth that all aspects of creation took

8 C. Vonk speaks of the "idea of rest" as being the "signature" of all of the feasts, not only of Sabbath. *De Voorzeide Leer: Leviticus*, vol. 1b (Uitgave: Drukkerij Barendrecht, 1963), 635.

their meaning and purpose from the One who called it into being. Sabbath thus became a gift that defined Israel's notion of work and gave her a sense of holy vocation. From her stewardship of beasts of burden to her management of servants and employees, Israel was to sense that she was a people on a peculiar mission in the name of her God. Noortzij observes: "The rhythmic character that the Sabbath gave to the Israelites' life, which is met with nowhere else in the ancient Near Eastern world, contributed to distinguishing them as a peculiar people, and it at the same time exerted an extremely favorable influence both on their capacity for work and on their manner of life in general."[9]

If the weekly Sabbaths became routine, every seventh year would jump-start an even stronger memory. Remembering creation was more than a mental exercise; God put legs and feet under the command. On Sabbath days, men and animals were to take a day off to taste God's gift of rest in their weary world, recalling that work was not supposed to be toil. But in Sabbath years, even the soil would be allowed to remember the goodness it once enjoyed before weeds choked the dirt or invaders salted it. All of creation, including its very soil, had once been good; it bore a divine voiceprint because it had been created by the word of the Lord.[10]

In a delightful portrait of faith and life in rural Iowa in the 1930s, poet Sietze Buning helps us understand a rest that touched all of creation:

> Into the daily swill of skim milk and cornmeal
> Dad stirred an extra number-two canful
> of Peet's Perfection Mineral Supplement
> on Saturday nights for the pigs' Sunday breakfast.
> It always foamed over the barrel by Sunday morning
> and turned so crusty on top you had to cut it with a spade.
> It was like slopping the pigs on Sunday with coffee cake.
> Roy, Bob, Frank, and Snoodles, our four horses,
> each got an extra gallon of oats on Sunday morning;
> every cow an extra half-gallon of shelled-corn meal;
> the chickens an extra gallon of shelled corn on the ground . . .

9 *Bible Student's Commentary: Leviticus* (Grand Rapids: Zondervan Publishing Corp., 1982), 230.

10 Walter Brueggeman, *The Land: Place as Gift, Promise, and Challenge in Biblical Faith* (Philadelphia: Fortress, 1977), 49.

Not even during threshing did our overweight horses
need extra oats, although they gladly feasted . . .

Dad's explanations:
"We look to God as animals look to us.
We're their idea of God, their image of God.
God's love to animals flows through us to them.
How will they know God's love unless we show them?
How can they tell the Lord's Day from another?
How can we comfort animals except by food?
They groan for eternal Sabbath with all creation."[11]

Deliverance flavored the second giving of the Sabbath command in Deuteronomy 5, adding a second nuance to all the Sabbaths. Deliverance must be remembered, too: Israel was to recall and retell the story of the patriarchs—and especially the story of the Exodus—to the rising generations. But it also involved wrestling in faith to see glimpses of the redemption to come more fully on a future day. For the Sabbaths tilted Israel forward to the coming Messiah, one who would finally bring authentic rest. His name was Jesus; all the Sabbaths of the Old Testament would find their meaning in him.

"Come to me, all you who are weary and burdened," he would cry, "and I will give you rest" (Matthew 11:28). In the very next verses, he called himself "Lord of the Sabbath," validating his claim by healing a man with a shriveled hand on the Sabbath day. Defiantly rejecting the Pharisees' demand that Sabbath be honored by the avoidance of work, he insisted that his work brought rest.

His rest did not come because he healed a man or plucked grain *on* a Sabbath day, thus offering people an example that stretched the traditional understanding of Sabbath behavior. The central teaching of Jesus about the Sabbath is that no one finds rest by his own efforts, by what Scripture calls "observing the law," even Sabbath laws. The Old Testament prohibition against work on the Sabbath—under penalty of death, no less (Exodus 31:15)—anticipated that truth. God wanted his people to know—in every generation—that seeking rest by their own effort was a doomed enterprise, for no rest is to be found at the end of such a quest. Thus he forbade them from working to find it.

11 "An Open Letter," in *Style and Class* (Orange City, Iowa: Middleburg Press, 1982), 56–7. Cited with permission.

Jesus' words and Jesus' Sabbath-keeping hung a neon sign in a public place, a sign for all generations to see: *Working at rest won't bring it—don't even try!*

Only God can give rest, and it will come only through Christ. God's rest would be secured by Jesus' death on the cross as a punishment for our sin and as the end of the guilt that makes our souls so very restless. Paul would instruct the Romans that Jesus "was delivered over to death for our sins" (4:25) and that "our old self was crucified with him so that the body of sin might be done away with, that we should no longer be slaves to sin" (6:6). He explained this more fully in his letter to the Galatians: "I have been crucified with Christ and I no longer live, but Christ lives in me" (2:20).[12] He assured them that, justified by faith, we have "peace with God" (Romans 5:1). His conclusion was that, in light of the cross of Christ, "there is now no condemnation for those who are in Christ Jesus" (8:1).

Such rest runs deep, for it releases our souls from the burden of guilt both for sins committed and obedience omitted, seals the tear in the fabric of our personal history, and gives each of us a new purpose and meaning that is tied to a new life enjoyed in the love of God.

Yet keen eyes and sensitive hearts know well that the restlessness of the world and in the human soul is not yet completely done away with. People still hurt, they still cry, and they still die, all marks of the old restless order of things.

> James and Rebecca were the model couple. Newly wed and in their late twenties, they are handsome, their wedding picture the sort that could have adorned frames for sale at the neighborhood Target. And with a new baby, life before them had a sweet cast to it. James had been a Navy diver, was well trained, and was physically a specimen the likes of which would inspire jealousy in all men over the age of forty. They were partners in a new business venture that promised a solid and prosperous future.
>
> But when James suffered nine days of relentless, brutal headaches, it was not only Rebecca who was concerned; the doctors shifted into diagnostic overdrive. They dug deep, ordering tests that bewildered and frightened everyone. The tests confirmed the worst fears: James had a brain tumor.

---

12 The verb tells the story: it is in the perfect tense, stressing completed action with ongoing results.

The diagnosis launched a series of bewildering but rapid interventions: immediate brain surgery was radical, but left massive scars; follow-up radiation targeted cancer cells with precision but destroyed healthy hair follicles as well; and chemotherapy attacked the disease broadly but brought a weariness for which young men are unprepared. Tears gave way to fears, and fears gave way to more tears as the unknown trumped the known. At first, the tumor was seldom discussed, a pink elephant everyone knows is in the room but which no one wants to acknowledge. Gradually, as they grew in faith, and with the support of family and friends, the tumor became a reality to be dealt with, a factor in daily life, but not the defining factor.

James and Rebecca are resting in Christ. Like all of us, they do not know the future. But if asked, they'll tell you, without hesitance, that all is well.

Stories like theirs remind us that there is an undeniable *not yet* to our rest in Christ. We inhabit a broken world; those who follow Christ walk with both a limp and a tilt, hobbled both by cosmic brokenness and by personal sin, always leaning toward the new order of things his resurrection promises. Even though people who come to Christ really do find forgiveness, joy, and hope because of the finished redemption his cross provides, they don't always heal completely—not this side of glory, anyway. Our sins don't disappear overnight; neither do their consequences. Some brain tumors are completely healed; but sometimes, the medical journey is a hard one and the outcome sad. Sinful marital patterns—twisted out of shape over decades—don't untangle easily; memories aren't quickly purged of cruel treatment or harsh words, and hearts cringe in desperate fear for years following physical or verbal abuse. One may be set free from addictions, but a rotten liver may well be the price of decades of overindulgence. A bright young mind may have limitless potential, but a self-image crippled by the cruel names children call out or damaged by parental criticism that never shows unconditional love or approval may well be hobbled for life—life this side of the grave, anyway.

We already taste rest, but we haven't yet been seated at the table for the full feast. "There remains, then, a Sabbath-rest for the people of God" (Hebrews 4:9).

Twisted Sabbaths, Weary Rest

Ever been invited to a party at someone's home, only to discover that there was no reason for the party? There is nothing to celebrate, nothing drawing this particular group of people together except the personalities of the hosts. In such gatherings, most mill around for a while, but leave early. With all due respect to the hosts, nothing keeps them there.

Parties without meaning are empty; they have no purpose other than fun, a pale counterfeit for real joy. The truth is that it is easy to lose the purpose of a celebration. A wedding anniversary can be shared with friends, with a first-rate dinner at a five-star restaurant and a card or gift, while the first love that bloomed into wedding vows shrivels after years of neglect, cold hearts, and quiet desperation. In our culture, Christmas commemorations are often the worst. Traditions like gift-giving—unrelated to the birth of Christ in Bethlehem of Judea but essential to the commercial extravaganza December 25 has become—drape the holidays with stress and financial pressures that make them prime time for painful family crises and bleak seasonal depression. In today's commercialized culture, the incarnate Son of God has become as easy to miss in December as a mustard seed in a shopping mall.

The meaning of the Sabbaths was easy to lose too. Over the centuries, Israel distorted the biblical gift of rest by reducing Sabbath to duty and tying it to a twenty-four-hour period beginning at dusk on Friday. She worked the day to death and "turned the permission to rest into an imperative."[13] She scrupulously obeyed the rules and drew out the implications but never found the rest the day proclaimed. She worked hard at not working: her rabbis identified "Sabbath day journeys" that limited the distance a person could walk without his steps becoming laborious. A housewife was permitted to take one stitch in a garment, but two constituted work and thus broke the law. Some knots might be tied on a Sabbath, but others—any that would be lasting knots, like a camel-driver's knot or a sailor's—were prohibited. If a stone lay on the mouth of a jar, the jar could be tipped so that the stone fell off. But the stone itself could not be lifted; such would constitute labor.[14]

Modern people react variously to the notion of Sabbath. Many ignore it altogether, giving the day no spiritual significance except as part of

13 Noortzij reminds us that the prohibition of all work was not absolute. *Leviticus*, 230.

14 For a glimpse at the extensive rabbinic tradition surrounding Sabbath laws, see Shabbath 15.1 in *The Mishnah*, trans. Herbert Danby (Oxford: Oxford University Press, 1933), 113.

a recreational weekend.[15] Some see no compelling connection between Sunday and the Sabbath. They reason that the age called Law is past and another called Grace has arrived, and with the change in epochs, Sabbath became a relic of the former dispensation.

Other Christian fellowships are convinced of a different logic: Sabbath is tied to the fourth of God's Ten Commandments. Sunday has replaced Saturday and is now the Christian Sabbath, and keeping the Sunday-Sabbath is a matter of obedience. Believers are to follow God's laws against unnecessary work or commerce on the Lord's Day.

Those who are eager to flee Sabbath legalism risk forgetting that Sabbath did not start out as a complex of rules but as a celebration of rest that echoed God's own joy in the sweet fellowship between a creation and its Creator. They also risk forgetting that Sabbath is a celebration of deliverance—first in the Exodus and now more fully in Christ. Such celebrations shaped two thousand years of the church's pattern of faith: she gathered communally each Sunday to rest in him.

On the other hand, those who suggest that rest can be attained by shifting Old Testament Sabbath proscriptions from Saturday to Sunday also run a risk. They risk forgetting that any rest that has to be obtained by human efforts—even Sabbath-keeping ones—is not really rest at all.

The hard part of honoring Sabbath today is sorting out what is rehearsal and what is truly feast, what was temporary and what is eternal, what is shadow and what is the substance that cast it (Colossians 2:17).

Such struggles are not new. John Calvin, the sixteenth-century reformer, wrestled with the same tensions, and provides a helpful perspective. He warns against "superstition" in regard to Sabbath-keeping:

> By the Lord Christ's coming the ceremonial part of this commandment was abolished. For *he himself is the truth*, with whose presence all figures vanish; he is the body, at whose appearance the shadows are left behind. *He is, I say, the true fulfillment of the Sabbath* . . . Christians ought therefore to shun completely the superstitious observance of days.[16]

15 Ironically, what our culture refers to as *recreation* (meaning by the term weekends, sports, and play) is rooted in the biblical concept of redemption, the bringing of the new creation—and with it, rest.

16 *Institutes of the Christian Religion*, ed. McNeill, bk. 2, chap. 8:32 (Philadelphia: The Westminster Press, 1967). Italics added.

In the same paragraphs in which Calvin argues that the "ceremonial part" of the fourth commandment should be abolished, he affirms two valid reasons for "observing Sabbath." The first is a call to gather "on stated days" for worship and instruction in God's Word, which will help us to rest in Christ and turn away from seeking to earn rest by the works of the flesh. The second is a call to treat employees well, giving them a day of rest to show the holistic grace the kingdom of God brings.[17]

Calvin's balanced warnings are fresh and timely for believers in this generation. Any view or practice of Sabbath that puts its focus on our behavior one day of the week instead of placing the focus on the accomplished work of redemption by grace in Christ is off target. Jesus Christ is the true Sabbath; all the Sabbath requirements in the Old Testament point to the rest he alone would provide for his people by the cross and resurrection. Learning to rest in the salvation that Jesus brought—without adding our own efforts—is the way we embrace Sabbath rest. All the weight of salvation is borne by Christ alone, given to us by grace alone, embraced by faith alone.

My wife and I recently enjoyed the privilege of a working sabbatical. I was working on this chapter, in fact, so Sabbath rest was in the forefront of my mind and heart. We were excited one Sunday when we visited another church and read in the bulletin that the preacher would preach about keeping Sabbath. Very articulate and most persuasive, he touched on important issues. He charged us to "get off the merry-go-round" of stress to find freedom from the tyranny of the urgent. He recited compelling statistics showing how busy we are as a culture and how desperately we need to find balance by taking time off from the demands of work. He lamented that our expanding list of labor-saving devices merely adds to our stress levels by seducing us to think we can get more done than ever.

But his solution—"Keep the Sabbath; take Sundays off!"—missed the mark. Not a word was spoken about resting *in Christ alone*. Not a word pointed us to the cross and the resurrection as the ground of our peace. Time management was offered as a substitute redeemer.

As we left, I couldn't help thinking that the same talk could have been delivered by an Orthodox Jew steeped in the Sabbath regulations of the Mishnah or a secular business consultant advising an overworked

17 Ibid., 8:32. For Calvin, Sunday has no special claim as the day of rest but is an accommodation to our weakness, only advisable because we do not worship every day. He comments, "Would that we were privileged to do so!"

client. Perhaps the word *Sabbath* would have appeared in the former's presentation and been absent from the latter's. Yet the message would have been the same: if you take a day off you will achieve schedule and relationship balance, find relief from over commitment, and be able to invest more time in marriage and family. The benefits will be well worth the effort.

Few will disagree that a day off can benefit stressed people and that renewing your commitment to a busy family shows love and provides nurture to a generation of children themselves showing the strain of this pressured life. But the currents of restlessness run deep, their source bubbling from places other than schedules. Going to church faithfully on Sundays does not itself fix the greed that drives people the other days. Making a commitment not to go shopping on Sunday or go to the office that day could be driven by a desire to honor the Lord more purely. But it may as well be driven by tradition, custom, or even fear of reprisal—from the Lord, your parents, or your church community. Ultimately, keeping Sabbath by such behavioral commitments one day a week is no guarantee at all that your rest is in Christ or that your labor the other six is "unto the Lord."

To find rest in a world of relentless change, stress, and the tyranny of the urgent, people need a new heart, one emptied of self-reliance and unburdened of frustrating duty, one desperate for God's grace. They need redemption of a kind that will set the world right once more.

The Sabbaths in Leviticus 23 showed the movement of the plot of God's redemption: he would bring rest to a restless world. But his redemption would prove to be something mysterious, different from anything Israel could imagine. In fact, it would take seven feasts to help her dream.

Questions for Further Study and Discussion

1. God established Sabbaths (plural) that blessed animals, servants, and even the land itself with rest. How does this fact shape your thinking about the redemption Christ brought?
2. Re-read Matthew 11:28–12:13. How does the healing of the man with a shriveled hand bring him Sabbath rest?
3. Hebrews 4:9 speaks of a Sabbath rest to come. Will it be a rest tied to a Saturday (Old Testament Sabbath), Sunday (called by many the Christian Sabbath), or neither?
4. Do you rest well in the cross and resurrection of Christ? Does your church? Talk about it.
5. The chapter refers to God's "relentless movement of history from restlessness to rest." How does this divine movement affect the way you engage the daily news reports? Does it shape the yearnings of your heart? Does it influence the mission strategy of your local church to bring rest to the restless in your community? Should it?

The Old Testament Festival Rehearsals

Dating According to Jewish Calendar

Sabbath

1. Passover (1st month, 14th day)
2. Unleavened Bread (1/15–21)
3. Firstfruits (1/16)
4. Weeks/Pentecost (3/6)
5. Trumpets (7/1)
6. Day of Atonement (7/10)
7. Booths (7/15–21)

Jubilee

Fulfilled in the Christ

Sabbath

His Earthly Ministry

Crucifixion/Passover (Friday)

Burial/Unleavened Bread (Saturday)

Resurrection/Firstfruits (Sunday)

From Throne As Ascended Lord

Pentecost/the Gift

Through His Church

Preaching the Gospel

The Joy of Salvation

Living Fellowship

Jubilee

A Gospel-Shaped People

Justified

Sanctified

New Creation

Empowered by Spirit

Witnesses to Gospel

Forgiven, Accepted

A New Community

Diagram 2.1: The Feasts

Chapter 2

BEHOLD THE LAMB!

THE FEAST OF PASSOVER

Leviticus 23:44–45 and Exodus 12

After the first two chapters of the Bible with its first two acts—*creation* and *fall*—the stage of history darkened ominously before the curtain rose on its third act, *redemption.* You may recall that one of the results of sin had been God-ordained "enmity," open warfare between the seed of the serpent and the seed of the woman. The ugliness of the conflict had become apparent immediately: from the brokenness of the lives of the first parents it soon spread to the next generation, erupting as violence between brothers. Cain killed Abel, revealing that the battle lines between faith and unbelief ran through the first family itself (Genesis 4).

Life goes on, even in a war zone. As time passed, men and women—both believers in God and those opposed to him—built culture and developed a world. They labored under the cultural mandate God had given Adam and Eve: subduing the earth, cultivating the simple to form the more complex, leveraging knowledge to develop the beautiful and the useful, but sometimes to develop the fearful and the ugly. Just a few verses (but many years) after the horrid story of Cain and Abel, we learn how diversified culture had become: we meet Jabal, the father of herdsmen; Jubal, the father of musicians; and Tubal-Cain, the father of metal workers.

They were Adam's heirs, culture-formers themselves, but the culture they developed was off-color and off-pitch, for their heart motives were self-centered rather than God-directed. In this they followed their father Lamech, an abuser who talked trash to keep his wives in line (Genesis 4:23–24).

Sin's power to corrupt warped all of creation. The diagnostic summary written early in the story of Noah pulls no punches: "The LORD saw how great man's wickedness on the earth had become, and that *every* inclination of the thoughts of his heart was *only evil all the time*" (Genesis 6:5, emphasis added). God judged that first world with a flood; but—as only God could do—he delivered a judgment that carried within it seeds of redemption. For the ark, sealed by God to keep the wicked out—thus assuring their destruction—also carried Noah and his family to safety. They were the hope of the future.

Through the rest of Genesis, the enmity played out like a soap opera—a nonfiction one. It got as dirty as street prostitution, catfights between competing lovers, and a lying mama's boy who pulled one over on daddy's favorite. History's lens zoomed in for a close-up to find twins from the same womb positioned on opposite sides of God and then panned wide for a war between kings and nations and a famine that enveloped the greatest culture of the day. By the end of the Bible's first book, the line of God's covenant had witnessed murder, adultery, betrayal, and deceit. Its heroes had proved to be anything but.

Yet God never wavered from his redemptive course, and by the close of the book, the fledgling line of Jacob had been brought to Egypt. God would use for good what Joseph's brothers intended for evil when they sold him into slavery, jealous of his birthday present.

Showdown at the Nile

In Egypt, God would incubate this infant people into a great nation. But the incubator malfunctioned; the benevolent Pharaoh who honored Joseph was soon replaced by one who forgot what Joseph had done. A people who had once feasted on the bounty of grace soon tasted the bitterness of bondage.

The enslavement of the children of Israel in Egypt was as complete as it was cruel. They were owned for life or death by Pharaoh. Exodus 1 tells the tale: reduced to "forced labor" (v. 11), driven by oppression, and motivated by the very real presence of death all around them, they were "used . . . ruthlessly" by the Egyptians (v. 14). And when the blessings of God burst forth in astounding birth rates for his slaves despite the abuse heaped upon them, Pharaoh simply pivoted and adopted a new game plan. He ordered infanticide.

Horrific as this was, the next chapters tell of an even more chilling reality: spiritually, the children of Jacob lost their identity. God had remembered his covenant promise: "God heard their groaning and he remembered his covenant with Abraham, with Isaac and with Jacob" (2:24). But the people of God completely forgot him. By the time Moses met God in the burning bush in Exodus 3, he had to ask, "Who are you?"

God answered, "I am who I am."

Moses asks for a little help: "Suppose I go to the Israelites and say to them, 'The God of your fathers has sent me to you,' and they ask me, "What is his name?' Then what shall I tell them?"

God patiently complies. "YHWH, the God of your fathers—the God of Abraham, the God of Isaac and the God of Jacob—has sent me to you. This is my name forever, the name by which I am to be remembered from generation to generation" (3:13, 15).

Now Moses has a name to tell the children of Israel—YHWH, a name that is more than a name. It is a powerful one-word sermon, one that serves both to identify and to proclaim: YHWH *means* "The One who is."[1] Moses is to go back to Egypt, he is to speak both to Israel and to Pharaoh, and he is to introduce YHWH as *the God who really* is over against the *gods who are not.*[2]

Moses did just that. He returned to Egypt to confront the divine god-king Pharaoh, force a showdown with the gods of the Egyptian pantheon, and call the people of Israel to follow YHWH to freedom. This set the stage for the ten plagues. Each was both apocalyptic evidence of divine outrage—"judgment on all the gods of Egypt" (Exodus 12:12)—and a gracious revelation of the God Who Is to the people of his heart.

To understand the plagues, it is important to be aware that the Egyptians, like the Canaanites Israel would soon face, thought their gods were territorial, possessing power only over limited areas or dimensions of the natural realm. YHWH met each on his own turf. None would be a match for a God who truly is.

---

1 YHWH, often spelled out as Yahweh or Jehovah, is usually translated in modern versions of the Bible as LORD, in capital letters. Jews, mindful of the third commandment, typically refer to God as HaShem, "the Name."

2 W. H. Gispen, *Bible Student's Commentary: Exodus* (Grand Rapids: Zondervan, 1982), 55.

The first plague turned the Nile to blood (Exodus 7:14–24); it was YHWH's opening body blow to the Egyptian god Hapi, the father of the gods and the territorial god over the Nile, the source of life for all Egypt. He then sent frogs (8:1–15), a scornful swipe at Heqt, the toad-goddess thought to be ruler of the land. The third plague of gnats (8:16–19) was like a flurry of jabs to the face of Geb, the idol of earth and vegetation. The fourth sent in waves of flies (8:20–32), a disorienting attack against Khepfi, believed to be the god of insect life.

The next plague (9:1–7) affected the livestock in the land and exposed the impotence of both Apis and Hathor, the bull-god and the cow-goddess of Egypt. The sixth brought boils to afflict both man and beast (9:8–12), a left hook on the chin of defenseless Thoth (Imhotep), a deity to whom Egypt turned for healing. The Egyptians sometimes burned human sacrifices alive, scattering the ashes to petition Thoth's favor. Moses knew the practice, having grown up in the Egyptian royal court. But now he knew YHWH, so he rubbed it in, mocking the no-god by scattering ashes that brought painful disease instead of healing it. The seventh plague, that of hail (9:13–35), destroyed all crops and laid waste to the supposed domain of Nut, the goddess of the sky whose rain was thought to bless the crops. With the eighth plague, locusts (10:1–20), YHWH finished off the destruction of Egypt's land and humiliated Anubis, god of the fields. And with the ninth, darkness so thick it could be felt (10:21–29), he turned lights out on the great Amon Re, the Sun-god and father of the pharaohs.

The tenth plague was the most terrible, a devastating knock-out blow (chapters 11–12). In it, YHWH brought "judgment on *all* the gods of Egypt." YHWH, the God Who Is, focused his justice on the Egyptian god-king Pharaoh, not only laying waste his present kingdom but also cutting off his dynasty by killing his firstborn, heir to the throne and a deity in his own right.

The History and Celebration of the Feast

Against the backdrop of these astonishing events, God established his Passover. It was a feast, to be sure, but it was a somber one. First of all the feasts in both sequence and significance, it embodied the heavy drama of redemption. In Passover God revealed the blood basis of his covenant with his people, showing that salvation would come only by death, only by the gracious substitution of a lamb. Passover would act out a painful truth: deliverance from sin's bondage would be costly. It would also embody hope: freedom would bring with it a new life and a new status. After Passover, the erstwhile slaves would become the sons of God.

Egypt: The Threshold of Freedom

As with all the feasts we will survey in these pages, we will learn that the centuries of Israel's life in Canaan witnessed developing festal traditions. Therefore, a thorough study will require a comparison between the original celebration prescribed at the base of Sinai and recorded in the Torah of Moses and the feast as it came to be celebrated in the centuries leading to the arrival of Messiah.

Passover was first celebrated on the day of Israel's departure from Egypt. Specific requirements given by Moses to the people of God and recorded in Exodus 12 shaped the festival:

- The guest list was intimate: it was a family-based celebration, each man selecting a lamb for his own household, sharing with a neighbor only if his family was too small to consume the whole.
- The menu was simple: a lamb, taken from the sheep or the goats, was to be a yearling "without defect" (Exodus 12:5), selected on the tenth day of the month but not slaughtered until the fourteenth, then roasted over a fire and consumed entirely; any leftovers were to be burned. Simple side dishes included bitter herbs and unleavened bread.
- The dress code was casual: the meal was eaten in traveling clothes and with staff in hand (Exodus 12:11).
- The "celebration" was bloody: the lamb was slaughtered above a small trench at the door of each home, its blood then smeared on the "sides and tops" of the doorframe, thus covering all four sides of the entrance.[3]

But bullet-point summaries of such a rich feast cannot tell the whole tale. As Israel observed the Passover in Egypt on the threshold of liberation, God was involving her in a much greater story. He had, only days before, introduced himself to his people with a mighty display of power when he destroyed the Egyptian gods. Now she would become much more than an objective observer, for Passover meant life or death to her as well. If she truly trusted in YHWH, she would live by the blood of the lamb. If she did not believe, if she did not mark her doors with its blood, her firstborn would die just as Egypt's firstborn did.

3 Ceil and Moishe Rosen, *Christ in the Passover* (Chicago: Moody Press, 1978), 31, note that "basin" in Exodus 12:22 was probably not a container in the sense we would use the word, tracing the etymology of the word to the Egyptian sap, meaning threshold or ditch dug in front of the doorway of the house to prevent seepage.

Under Moses' strong leadership, Israel trusted, her faith actively responding to YHWH, actively embracing the God Who Is with every one of her senses. Her eyes wide as she actively scrutinized the lamb for defects; her hands stained from slaughtering the lamb and smearing its blood; her ears ringing with the screams of dying animals; her nostrils filled with the stench of death and the fragrance of roasting meat; and her mouth savoring every morsel of the feast that followed.

The elements of the feast would thus serve to introduce Israel to who she was in God's eyes. The bitter herbs would remind her of her own story, of centuries of cruel oppression and harsh tyranny. The unleavened bread would tell another story, a tale of a new beginning, a break with the miserable past and an entrance into a radically new and different life. Central to the feast was the lamb, a dying substitute for a people's life. Its lifeblood, smeared on doorposts and lintel, would serve to testify of the love of God for the people of his heart. She had not been forgotten in Egypt; God had heard her cries, and he had answered. He had "covered" his people from the justice brought by the angel of death. Even the name of the feast bore great meaning and told the gospel story: *pesach*, the Hebrew word for Passover, is rooted in the Egyptian term *pesh*, a term that portrays the vivid image of a God who "spread wings over" his people in order to protect and save them.[4]

A New Life: Canaan

Commemoration of the Passover in the desert ceased after only two festivals. No surprise, I guess. A grumbling spirit doesn't party well; it pouts instead. Passover celebrations would not resume until Israel camped at Gilgal on the plains of Jericho (Joshua 5:10) some thirty-nine years later.

Passover practices soon adapted to Israel's new life in Canaan. She was no longer nomadic. She now lived in the land where God was king; the tabernacle, and later temple, would serve as the seat of his throne. Following instructions given in Deuteronomy 16:1–8, just before she crossed the Jordan into Canaan, Israel shifted her celebration of

4 The same word is used again in Isaiah 31:5. "Like birds hovering overhead, the LORD Almighty will shield Jerusalem; he will shield it and deliver it, he will 'pass over' it and will rescue it." It is likely that the term is also the basis for Jesus' tender lament in Luke 13:34: "O Jerusalem, Jerusalem . . . how often I have longed to gather your children together, as a hen gathers her chicks under her wings." Also see Arthur W. Pink, *Gleanings in Exodus* (Chicago: Moody Press, n.d.), cited in Rosen, 22.

the Passover from a family-based festival, once eaten in haste and in traveling clothing, to one more communal, now based "in the place he will choose as a dwelling for his Name." Only there could lambs be slain. This shift effectively made Passover the first of the "pilgrimage festivals" requiring Israel to journey to the house of the Lord.

We do not know much about Israel's Passover practices in the centuries under the kings. The feast is mentioned in the rest of the Old Testament only in connection with revivals that occurred under Josiah (2 Kings 23:21–22; 2 Chronicles 35:1–17) and Hezekiah (2 Chronicles 30). When God sent Nebuchadnezzar to sack the temple and take Israel to Babylon over five centuries later, Passover celebrations ceased completely until the exiles returned (Ezra 6:19).

Passover in the First Century

After the exile, and during the four hundred years between the testaments, the celebration of the Passover developed a growing complex of traditions. By the first century, Passover had merged with the Feast of Unleavened Bread until the two were commingled. Since these two festivals and a third one, the Feast of Firstfruits, took place in the space of three days, pilgrims would travel to Jerusalem once for all three. Luke, writing to a Greek audience, reflects the *de facto* merging of the feasts when he writes "now the Feast of Unleavened Bread, called the Passover, was approaching" (Luke 22:1).

Festival traditions developed for all aspects of the feast. The first notable shift in the first-century Passover involved a swirl of activities that surrounded the examination of the lamb. Recall that the Passover lambs were to be scrutinized to assure that they were without blemish. Whether these were lambs to be eaten in family gatherings or the one for the nation to be offered in the temple, by the first century, all animals for sacrifice were examined by priests serving in Herod's temple. Sacrifices could be brought in to the temple from the outside, of course, but they would have to pass under the gaze of the priests before slaughter. Most people bought their sacrifice from certified stock for sale at the temple. The hard lesson of a corrupt system was that the priests could—and did—find minute imperfections in virtually any lamb brought from the outside; the purchase of a lamb from "approved" stock was the only safe way to go.

The original family focus of the Passover celebration was not completely lost. Companies of ten to twenty adults would still constitute a "family" sufficient to consume an entire lamb. A rabbi and his disciples, like Jesus and the Twelve, would also satisfy the requirement.

But in the first century, the companies or family groups would present their lambs at the temple, where, at the sound of a silver trumpet on the fourteenth of Nisan, the priests would slit the throats of the sacrificed lambs, catching the blood in basins so that it could later be poured out at the base of the altar. At the time of sacrifice, a levitical choir chanted the great Hallel, Psalms 113–118, while the congregation antiphonally replied "Hallelu-Yah!"—"Praise the LORD!"

The companies of ten to twenty would then return to their homes or meeting places to eat the lamb in the traditional Seder ("order of service") meal. In this meal, the Hallel Psalms would again form the structure for the meal, while the specific food items and the four cups of wine served to give it a redemptive focus.[5]

- The opening *Kiddush*, or blessing, was recited over the first cup of wine—the cup of *blessing*—after which water was poured over the hands of the host in a ceremonial washing.
- *Karpas*, a bitter form of lettuce or parsley, was the first food brought in; it was dipped into salt water or vinegar and passed to each participant. The second cup of wine—the cup of *wrath*—was poured, but not yet drunk. The youngest son was ready for his moment: he asked (Exodus 12:26) "What does this night mean?" and the host father recited the bitter history of Israel's bondage and deliverance from Egypt. The cup of wrath was drunk.
- The remaining food (lamb, bitter herbs, and unleavened bread) was then served as the assembly sang the first part of the Hallel (Psalm 113–114), songs that celebrated YHWH's deliverance from Egypt. Following another blessing, the feast was consumed. The host broke and distributed unleavened bread (*matzo*). It was dipped in *maror* bitter herbs, probably ground horseradish, either alone or mixed with bitter lettuce, endive, or coriander—to recall the bitterness of bondage, and *haroseth*, a mixture of chopped apples, spices, and nuts, representing the mortar of Israel's hard brickwork in Egypt. Finally, they ate the lamb that was reminiscent of their salvation.
- After the meal, the third cup—the cup of *redemption*—was poured and drunk. The rest of the Hallel Psalms (115–118) were sung or recited. These psalms of praise looked back and voiced the people's gratitude for redemption accomplished.

5 For a fuller description of the first-century Seder, see Ceil and Moishe Rosen, 50–59.

- Finally, the fourth cup—the cup of the *kingdom*—was poured and drunk, and the Seder came to an end with a song that looked forward. That song began, "All thy works shall praise thee, YHWH our God," and ended, "From everlasting to everlasting Thou art God, and beside Thee, we have no King, Redeemer or Savior."

In addition to the family Seder, Passover celebrations in the first century were also commemorated publicly and corporately in a somber and impressive ceremony in the temple courtyard over which the high priest himself presided. This public Passover had its own complex of traditions. Several days before the day of Passover, on the tenth of Nisan, as prescribed by Exodus 12:3, the "lamb for the people" was put on public display in the courtyard of the temple for examination by all. At 9:00 a.m. on the fourteenth of Nisan, and as backdrop to the sacrifice of the thousands of lambs for family-sized celebrations,[6] the high priest led that lamb for the people to the altar, where it was "staked out"—tied to a post to await slaughter at the time of the evening sacrifice. When the time came, at or shortly before 3:00 p.m., the lamb for the people was slain, its throat slit and its blood collected while the high priest recited the liturgical formula for a peace offering.

Behold the Lamb!

Jesus, a rabbi of the first century, kept the feast as it had come down to his generation, a celebration wrapped in centuries of customs. He honored all the requirements of a traditional Passover celebration. His Last Supper was obviously a Seder meal.

But Jesus did more than keep the feast. He *embodied* it. John the Baptist had once introduced Jesus with words that borrowed imagery from the Passover feast: "Behold, the lamb of God, who takes away the sin of the world" (John 1:29 ESV). His words were more true than even he knew.

A Lamb without Blemish

In a requirement dating back to Exodus 12:5 and its earliest celebrations, the Passover lamb had to be "without blemish." This question was the first to be settled before Jesus could lay claim to be the Lamb of God. The examinations of this Lamb were many, and they were rigorous. And at the end of each, Scripture records the verdict.

6 It is estimated that the regular population of Jerusalem in the first century was six hundred thousand. The pilgrims who filled the streets during festivals swelled the population to two million or more.

The first trials of the Lamb were public and were conducted under the prosecution of the Pharisees and the Sadducees, the two religious parties of the day. Jesus entered the city of Jerusalem in the frenzy of the triumphal entry. On the next day, and at the same time and place that the "lamb for the people" was initially put on public display in the temple courtyard, Jesus presented himself to the chief priests, the teachers of the law, and the elders for their scrutiny. They grilled him rigorously, particularly about his authority to perform miracles (Mark 11:27–33), but he exposed their wicked motives, thus invalidating their judgment. The Pharisees and Herodians next tried to trap him with a trick question about taxes and loyalty to Caesar (Mark 12:13–15); he left them slack-jawed with his simple answer. Scripture simply records "they were amazed at him" (v. 17). The Sadducees next took a swing (12:18–27), but whiffed. Jesus exposed their ignorance of Scripture. The Pharisees came back for more (Matthew 22:34–46), but left confounded.

Following all these public examinations of the Lamb, Scripture records the verdict: they found no fault in him. And, as a result, "No one could say a word in reply, and from that day on no one dared to ask him any more questions" (Matthew 22:46).[7]

The second examinations were more formal, shifting to the courtrooms of men officially charged with truth and justice. His first trial (John 18:13) took place before Annas, father-in-law of Caiaphas, but apparently the power behind the robes. He questioned Jesus about "his disciples and his teaching" (John 18:19). Whatever charges there were did not stick (John 18:23). Annas then sent him to Caiaphas (Matthew 26:57), who concluded that Jesus had committed blasphemy (v. 65), an obvious rush to judgment: none of the witnesses against him were valid, for none met the standards of the law (v. 60).

The trial turned next to the civil court of Pilate, the Roman governor. After questioning Jesus, he pronounced him innocent. There was "no basis for a charge against him" (John 18:38). No crime had been committed, and there was no ground for punishment. Pilate, surely no stranger to political intrigue, was bothered by the proceedings; he washed his hands of the whole affair on the advice of an overwrought wife.

Nonetheless he delivered Jesus over to be crucified, an obvious malfeasance of office, yet one that served the cause of the gospel.

7 The sequence of verdicts is reported in Mark 11:31–33; 12:17; 12:27; 12:32-34; Matthew 22:46.

For the last examination of the Lamb, the most decisive, was still to be conducted. It would be heard not in a human court but before the heavenly bench of God himself. The prosecutors were many, and they were thirsty for blood. There was no advocate for the defendant; he would have to speak for himself.

The "courtroom" was filled with high drama. In a bizarre twist, the accused was already on the cross, nailed to its beams at 9:00 a.m., precisely the time the lamb for the people was to have been staked out. The prosecutors—the chief priests and the teachers of the law—were ready to make their closing argument. Convinced they had the case in hand, they employed the technique of mockery. More than "sticks and stones," mockery intended to ridicule, to "make fun of someone by pretending that he is not what he is."[8] These tormentors stabbed at Jesus, citing a litany of quotations from the well-known messianic Psalm 22, aiming to prove that he was ***not*** the Messiah, for he could save neither himself nor others. Matthew's gospel contains the court reporter's record (compare Matthew 27:39 with Psalm 22:7; Matthew 27:42–43 with Psalm 22:8).

Jesus absorbed their words into his very soul even as his body absorbed the compounded agony of the flogging, the nails, and the crown of thorns. His response was tortured, each breath a painful struggle as he strained against his own diaphragm in the slow suffocation for which Roman crucifixions were known. When at last he gasped words, he chose them from the same psalm they had quoted against him: "My God, my God, why have you forsaken me?" (22:1). The supreme irony was that his claim to be Messiah ***could not*** be validated by stepping down from the cross, as they demanded, but only by bearing the focused wrath of God in place of his people. His quotation from the messianic psalm was his simple defense. It meant, "I am Messiah, indeed."

The final verdict came in. Creation's God himself declared it with a cosmic upheaval: the temple curtain was torn from top to bottom, an earthquake rent the land and broke the rocks, and a resurrection of the dead ripped open the graves (Matthew 27:51–53). The centurion and his guards added an exclamation point: "Surely he was the Son of God!" (27:54).

---

8 Johannes P. Louw and Eugene Albert Nida: *Greek-English Lexicon of the New Testament: Based on Semantic Domains,* electronic ed. (New York: United Bible Societies, 1996). S. 1:434.

God had once instructed Israel (Exodus 12:46): "Do not break any of the bones" of the Passover lamb. Clueless of the prophecy they were fulfilling, the execution squadron complied, departing from the Roman practice of breaking the legs of the crucified to assure the demise of a man stubbornly clinging to life. Instead, they pierced his side with a spear to prove that he was already dead. Even this unique post-mortem, which left the Lamb's bones intact, validated that he was, according to all the requirements of the law, a spotless lamb.

That he was a lamb "without blemish" was settled. How this Lamb's sacrifice would save his people becomes the question at hand.

The Body and the Blood

In the Seder meal, the third cup of *redemption* provided the central moment. Jesus took up the unleavened bread, dipped it in the bowl of wrath and sorrow, and announced in words quoted regularly in sacramental observances the world over: "Take it; this is my body" (Mark 14:22). In this one mysterious phrase, Jesus focused the gospel of the ages upon himself. He would take in his body the wrath of God that should fall on you and me, absorbing it in Gethsemane and especially on the cross. He would embrace all the misery of injustice, the unrighteousness of the ages, even the curse of death that has dogged God's people from the sweat yards of Egypt up to the present day.

Moments later, Jesus would pour and pass the cup. Once more he would preach a sermon, the content of which was himself: "This is my blood of the covenant, which is poured out for many" (Mark 14:24).

The blood on the lintels and frames of the doors of Goshen so many years before had anticipated this moment, for the blood that "covered" the people then was a rehearsal of this greater atonement. God's righteous anger would be appeased once and for all through the shedding of the blood of this Lamb. God is just; yet all who believe in the Lamb of God find mercy in the substitute.

That he died, and that his death was physically, psychologically, and spiritually horrific tell only part of the story. *When* he died completes the tale.

The timing of the day was rich with meaning. As noted earlier, the lamb for the people had been staked out at 9:00 a.m. At the same time that the high priest was tying off the frisky four-footed beast, Jesus was nailed to the cross on the other side of the wall before the eyes of the watching world. Later in the afternoon, at the traditional time for the slaughter of the "lamb for the people," the high priest cut its throat, concluding the peace offering with the standard liturgical proclamation,

"It is finished." But, *at the very same time*, on the other side of the wall, Jesus, the priest presiding over his own sacrifice, also cried out, "It is finished!" and breathed his last (Mark 15:37; Matthew 27:45–50). Jesus did not merely keep the Feast of Passover. He took it over.

The Gospel in the Feast

Passover was, as we saw in chapter 1, a rehearsal. In compelling typology, the shadows of Christ's redemption once flickered on the mud brick walls in Egypt, lit by events that would not occur for many long years. Those early shadows in the Old Testament revealed indistinct but identifiable shapes of God's truth; the Light that cast them clarified the lessons. Some were hard, others sweet.

Sin

The first lesson was about sin. Passover exposed sin as something far more than personal errors or moral failures, but as a power that holds people in bondage. Ancient Israel's daily grind was lived under Pharaoh's thumb. He owned her; she was his labor pool and her babies no more than replacement workers. When the Israelites became too numerous, they became a threat. Exodus 1 tells Pharaoh's grisly solution: he had them killed.

Sin is no less a slave master today. Hearts, minds, ethics, and lives are cruelly controlled in its powerful grip. Many of us are aware of sins, violations of specific laws of God that stain our lives. We covet our neighbor's SUV, even though gasoline is pricey and we couldn't afford to drive such a vehicle even if we had one. We justify lust, even if we do not commit full-blown adultery, in the belief that it is a no-harm foul; but we know better. Lies come easily in an age of marketing manipulation and political "spin"; the bigger challenge is actually telling the whole truth.

But not as many of us recognize that *Sin* (with a capital S) is the power behind *sins*. Sin enslaves, as surely as an addict is controlled by his addiction. Ephesians 2:1–3 vividly portrays life in sin as the need to feed the compulsions and "gratify the cravings."

> David had struggled for years with pornography. He knew in his soul that porn was an ugly counterfeit for real love. He also knew that his frequent use of it did not please God, but he played mental games, trying to convince himself that it was just a harmless hobby. The despair on his face when he learned that his porn addiction would cost him his marriage and destroy his relationship with his children was beyond describing. He wept, great sobs heaving his shoulders. He was undone.

Yet, the next weekend, he bought a new computer with a faster graphics card so he could feed his porn habit in the flophouse motel he had rented after his wife threw him out.

Sin-as-power distorts other dimensions of life as well, like our physical requirement for food and water. Drunkenness and gluttony are sins easy to name, but the power that drives them is profound. Anorexia, bulimia, and cutting reflect addictive patterns that are difficult to understand and even harder to break. Sin's control over people is so great as to expose as silly the notion of a will that is truly free.

Passover showed Israel—and us—that sin enslaves, and its bondage is cruel. It is bitter and joyless because it strips life both of freedom and of hope. Passover also showed that bondage is costly. Liberation can come only by death—not only that of a lamb but also of the idols our foolish hearts cherish in place of the only true God. For the LORD is jealous for our love: to break sin's death-grip, he had once destroyed the no-gods of the Egyptian pantheon. Today, the counterfeits our hearts cherish, counterfeits that enslave our lives, fall under his judgment too. He simply loves us too much to allow sin to deceive us into believing that real and satisfying life is possible apart from him.

Grace

Passover rehearsed the sweet lessons of redemption too. In the first place, it gave an early taste of grace as the driving power in salvation. Passover showed that redemption is not based on the efforts of those in bondage—no knowledge or behavior on our part will make right what sin has made wrong—but by the substitution of another. Israel did nothing to bring about her liberation. Salvation came only because God "remembered his covenant." Stuttering Moses was no savior; he was only the human messenger of the God Who Is who saved by his own mighty strength.

Grace was the force then, and grace is the operative dynamic for those who trust in Christ today. "For it is by grace you have been saved, through faith—and this not from yourselves, it is the gift of God—not by works, so that no one can boast" (Ephesians 2:8–9).

Atonement

Passover further defines atonement, a concept that had appeared earlier in the biblical story (as for example in the test of Abraham recorded in Genesis 22). Literally a "covering with blood," it visually portrays the redemptive overshadowing of God's people as if by the tender wings of a mother hen. Passover was not a primitive and ancient blood ceremony that demonstrates an ancient Bible's irrelevance to a modern world. In fact, just the opposite is true. The festival introduces a loving God who dealt personally with the very real consequences of our guilt, a lamb in place of men, so that men would never be required to spill their own blood to pacify an angry God. Nowhere is God's love more visible than in the death of Jesus, the Lamb of God—the very *Son* of God—who died to make enemies into sons.

Justification

Passover enacts justification by faith. While Scripture is clear that the eternal love of God is the originating cause of our redemption (John 3:16; Ephesians 1:4), it is also clear that in space and time, the death of the Lamb is ground zero, a fountain with many rivulets flowing from it. Justified by the death of the Lamb in their place, believers find their God instead of guilt and fear, and this grace empowers them to live a life of holiness and instills in them the desire and joy of worship.

Freedom

Passover also anticipates the joyous transformation of life by the gospel of Christ, for in the blood of the Lamb, God's people find liberty. More than mere freedom *from* sin, gospel liberty always brings a freedom *unto* a new life.

The harbinger of freedom appeared early in the Passover narrative. God had made an unexpected declaration when he established the Feast: "This month is to be for you the first month, the first month of your year" (Exodus 12:2). God did something only an absolute monarch had the right to do: he reset the calendar, announcing to a people long structured by the agricultural calendar of the Egyptians that life would start anew with their liberation. The seasons would not change, nor the cycles of planting and reaping that traced them; but overlaid upon those seasons and cycles was a new reality. Israel was to remember—with each yearly celebration of the Feast of Passover—that her existence as the people of God began with *God's* mighty deliverance from slavery.

In ancient times, slaves were often tied together in long lines, bound by neck chains, and even by lines attached to fish hooks driven through the cheek, a horrific practice that lay behind Amos' fearful prophecy (4:2). But individuals could be purchased out of the slave line, set free from the chains by the payment of a price. The biblical root word *redeem* has its roots in that practice. Redemption describes something much greater than physical emancipation. Redemption brings liberty from sin, from guilt, and from shame, the unholy triumvirate of co-conspirators that plot to rob people of joy and peace. Peter says pointedly, "You were redeemed from the empty way of life handed down to you from your forefathers . . . with the precious blood of Christ, a lamb without blemish or defect" (1 Peter 1:19).

Laura was twelve when her mother gave her to a boyfriend for sex in payment of a small debt. It didn't take long before Laura learned to hate herself, hate him, and trust no one. Yet, in the twisted logic of abuse victims, Laura soon discovered a survival skill: she could use men even as they used her. She became a stripper, and sex became the vocabulary of her interaction with men. It was a way she could control them rather than be controlled, a substitute for real love that made her feel wanted and accepted. It was a way to survive the hurts within.

When a co-worker told Laura of the love of Christ, she scoffed. Her mother had been religious, even though her religious practice was a cruel mockery of a living relationship with God. Soon, however, Laura became strangely transfixed by the stories the co-worker told of a God who loved so deeply, so intimately, so relentlessly that you could actually trust him with the deep places of your heart and tell him your secrets.

Laura showed up at church one day. She walked up to the counter and told the church secretary, in a voice shockingly free of emotional affect, that she was a stripper, wanted to quit, and needed a church that would help her turn her life around. God was clearly moving in her soul.

Unknown to her, God had been stirring in the secretary's heart too. She and her husband had become convicted of spiritual complacency and wanted to break out of the comfort zone of a risk-free life. She had been praying for weeks that God would grant them the spiritual boldness to live for Christ with radical obedience.

You can imagine Laura's surprise when the secretary said, without missing a beat, "Come live with my family!" (You can also imagine her husband's reaction when she came home with a stripper.) The family loved her with grace and mercy, testifying with words and deeds to the love of the Savior. That love began to transform Laura. She began to study the Word, attend worship, and soon began to give clear evidence of a life-changing faith in Christ. She experienced a joy so profound that she began to speak of her "personal BC and AD," calling her coming to Christ a second birthday, the reset of the calendar of her life.

Sonship

The gospel of Passover not only announces liberty, but also informs us that our new life will be lived as sons of God. God would explain the Exodus many years later in the words of his prophet Hosea: "out of Egypt I called my son" (Hosea 11:1). This new status belonged not only to an ancient people, but is the joyous identity of all who trust in Christ today. The apostle John exults: "To all who received him, to those who believed in his name, he gave the right to become children of God" (John 1:12). Paul is equally explicit: "Those who are led by the Spirit of God are sons of God. For you did not receive a spirit that makes you a slave again to fear, but you received the Spirit of sonship. And by him we cry, 'Abba, Father.' The Spirit himself testifies with our spirit that we are God's children. Now if we are children, then we are heirs—heirs of God and co-heirs with Christ" (Romans 8:14–17).

Glorious words, those; yet hard to believe when you were traded by your own mother for a debt and made your living as a stripper. Some never grasp the radical freedom of redemption. They prefer to return to the familiar cadence of the slave master. It feels more like home.

Free at Last?

Israel was like that. Freed from bondage, she soon looked over her shoulder, longing to return for the graves and the "leeks, onions and garlic" of her harsh life (Exodus 14:11-12; Numbers 11:5). The known was comfortable, if bitter; it was the unknown of her new freedom that was terrifying. Had Moses allowed it, she would have crawled back that first day.

People new to freedom, like Laura, are often similarly tormented by their new status when they know it is undeserved. We are, all of us, more at home with the familiar equations of moral accounting: we keep records, long lists of behavioral credits and debits, grading ourselves and judging others by the bottom line of what our behavior deserves. We've become so accomplished at the game that the audit-finding of the prodigal seems final: "I'm not worthy to be called your son" (Luke 15:19). So we live like slaves; freedom is foreign turf for those who have never known anything but bondage.

James Clavell's book *King Rat* was based on his personal experiences as a prisoner of war in a Japanese camp in Malaya at the close of World War II. Conditions in the camp were so desperate, food so scarce, that the starving prisoners would do anything to eat. The main character, Corporal King, devised a scheme to barter food for profit, hoping to keep himself and his fellow prisoners alive to the end of the war.

An American entrepreneur at heart, King was a mover and shaker within the confines of the camp, taking great satisfaction in the personal conviction that he could scam anyone, even the guards. Convincing everyone that he had access to scarce and precious "mouse deer," he generated exorbitant profits from the sale of the meat.

All was not what it seemed. In a macabre twist, King's "mouse deer" turned out to be rat meat; worse, it was the flesh of rats fattened by the corpses of dead prisoners. Horrible as this revelation was, it was only the beginning of King's demise. When the camp was liberated, King fell apart. What would he do now? Although his scheme had been devised to keep himself and others alive until freedom came, freedom itself was the greater foe. In the camp, King had been special; once freed, he was nothing, a nobody.

In Milton's *Paradise Lost*, Satan explains the twisted logic: "Better to reign in Hell, than serve in Heaven."

God still sets people free, and the gospel of Jesus the Messiah announces the liberation. It is a freedom to live and not just to survive, the freedom of an erstwhile slave who has become a son. Yet, unless you trust in Christ and embrace his death as your deliverance, you will never know such freedom. You will never experience the joy of sonship.

The shift from slave to son requires a transformation so radical as to defy logic. It would need more than a new attitude. It would require the death of the old ways and the birth of an entirely new life.

Questions for Further Study and Discussion

1. The chapter argues that the plagues described in the early chapters of Exodus contrast the impotent idols of Egypt with the powerful God Who Is. One modern cultural historian identifies some modern idols that usurp God's place in our hearts: some are idols of history (trust in the gradual but inevitable progress of humanity), idols of Mammon (faith in economic systems that offer money, investments, and wealth as the basis for our security), or idols of power (trust in the State to save us from harm or poverty, or in education to assure success, or science/medicine to provide us a longer life).[9] Why are such idols still no-gods, still impotent to save?
2. Read again the section of the chapter that explains the trials of Jesus, looking up each Scripture reference included. Why was it so important for Jesus to be validated as a "lamb without blemish"?
3. Read Romans 3–5. Try to write a concise definition of *justification.* Why is justification the heart of the *good news* of Jesus Christ? How is justification the fountain of Christian worship and joy?
4. How is a son's self-image different from a slave's? How is a son's inheritance different from a slave's? How should redemption in Christ affect your self image?

9 Herbert Schlossberg, *Idols for Destruction: Christian Faith and Its Confrontation with American Society* (Nashville: Thomas Nelson, Inc.), 1983.

Chapter 3

Cleaning House
The Feast of Unleavened Bread

Leviticus 23:6–8

A number of years ago, a friend gave me some advice. A widower for a few years, I was planning to marry again; he had been through similar circumstances some years earlier and figured correctly that I needed perspective. After congratulating me on my engagement, his counsel came in the form of a question: "The two of you are not going to live in your house after the wedding, are you?"

I was a little surprised by his query, because I had contemplated doing just that. After all, even though two years had turned the family home into a bachelor pad, my son having returned from college to become my roommate, it wasn't completely beyond reclamation. Besides, the idea seemed economical. My friend patiently explained that bringing a new bride into a home that had been furnished with love by another woman would create an impossible situation. My new wife couldn't redecorate without offending family members who cherished the mementos and photos of family celebrations in which she had no part, and yet these things would remind her that she was an outsider. Not to redecorate would be as bad: she would be saddled with the detritus of a past that would render her utterly incapable of establishing a new home and a new life.

My friend's counsel to me was simple and pointed. "Sell the house, give the furniture away, and make a clean break with the past."

He was talking about leaven.

The History and Ceremony of the Feast

The Feast of Unleavened Bread commenced the day after the Passover. The lamb had been slain and eaten in the somber ceremonies of that feast. The next day, a Sabbath, would began the new festival, one that would last a full week and build on the joy Passover initiated.[1]

According to the Torah (Leviticus 23:6–8), the Feast of Unleavened Bread was anchored by several traditional elements. Of course there was food. Israel's families ate unleavened bread, matzo, daily. A mere side dish in the Passover feast, it became the central element of the next week and the next feast. In addition, the festival was bracketed by two public "sacred assemblies," one on the Sabbath immediately after Passover, and the other on the Sabbath a week later. Like Passover, Unleavened Bread began as a family-based celebration, later shifting to a communal celebration at the house of the LORD after Israel entered the land of Canaan.

Key to the celebration of the feast was a living tension, one that stretched God's people between positive and negative commands. On the one hand, the feast embodied a positive command: Israel "must" eat the unleavened matzo each day. On the other, observing the feast involved a serious negative: Israel was to remove all leaven from her homes. Leaven, in the ancient world, was not the prepackaged yeast of our supermarkets, but rather active and bubbling starter from previous batches of dough. Leaven, for the purposes of the festival, meant more, including *anything* that had been leavened, even the smallest crumbs. Exodus 12:15 specified that on the first day of the feast Israel was "to remove the yeast from your houses, for whoever eats anything with yeast in it from the first day through the seventh must be cut off from Israel." This was serious business: "cut off" is covenant language for death.

The urgency of the language makes more sense if you remember the situation in which Israel found herself as she readied to depart Egypt. She ate the Passover meal in haste while dressed in traveling clothes because the judgment of God would soon fall on the gods of Egypt. In fact, her new life was set against the cries of death throughout

1 John Ritchie argues that the one-day feasts (Passover, Firstfruits, Weeks, and the Day of Atonement) focus on specific acts of redemption, while the seven- and eight-day celebrations point to the continuing outcome of these acts. *Feasts of Jehovah* (Grand Rapids: Kregel Publications, 1982), 33–34.

the land. The "first day" of the Feast of Unleavened Bread would be moving day, the departure day of the journey known as the exodus. Making sure no leaven was in their houses would serve as visible testimony of their faith and trust in God. It would certify that they were taking nothing of Egypt with her, that no living power of the enslaved past would make the journey with a people newly freed.

Forty long and difficult years later, the people of Israel finally crossed the Jordan to gather at Gilgal on the plains of Jericho. Egypt was, by this time, a distant memory. Israel was in Canaan now, and, except for Caleb and Joshua, none of the generation that had walked out of Egypt was still alive. The death of the previous generation had created a break with the past, full of painful memories of sin and disobedience. Upon entry into their new homeland and under Joshua's direction, the people's celebration of the feast would embody a liturgical break with the past: "the day after the Passover . . . they ate some of the produce of the land: unleavened bread and roasted grain. The manna stopped the day after they ate this food from the land" (Joshua 5:11–12). That day was the Feast of Unleavened Bread.

House Cleaning

No other celebrations of the Feast of Unleavened Bread are recorded in the remaining books of the Old Testament. Yet over the long centuries of Israel's history, and especially in the time between the testaments, the command to "remove the yeast from your houses" grew into a family custom that would illustrate the central meaning of the feast. This practice maintained the character of the feast as rehearsal, a shadow-type of the redemption of Messiah to come. It would also, like the Passover, include a teaching moment. The Passover Seder invited a son to ask his father, "Why is this night different?" The teaching moment within Unleavened Bread was known as *Bedikat HaMetz*, the purging of leaven from the house.

The custom involved the whole family and actually began, not on the first day of the festival as prescribed by Exodus 12:15, but a whole week earlier. After regular house cleaning, Mom would deliberately leave several small pieces of leavened bread scattered about the home, larger ones in easy view for the little ones, smaller pieces in harder-to-find places for older ones up to the challenge. Dad would then lead the adventure. Utilizing a candle, a wooden spoon, a feather, and a piece of linen cloth, the family would search diligently until they had found each piece. The excited children giggled with delight at each discovery until they were hushed by the father, who, carefully and with dramatic relish, swept the leaven into the spoon with the feather—no one was allowed to touch it—as if he were defusing a powerful explosive. To punctuate the seriousness, all the crumbs would later be burned.

More Than Breadcrumbs

This was no mere game; the drama taught an important lesson. "Children," their parents would dramatically intone, "leaven stands for the idolatry and influence of Egypt which God told us to leave behind when he brought us out by the blood of the lamb. Don't ever forget!" The lesson was sound, for the inquisitive children of the Israelites would soon discover that although Egypt was in the distant past, the power of leaven was alive and still dangerous in her new life in the land of Canaan. There she would meet the Ba'als.

The ten plagues had reduced the richest culture in the ancient world to something that resembled the surface of the moon. God's divine judgment had completely devastated Egypt and exposed her counterfeit gods. But the lesson of the plagues had been especially directed at Israel; God was jealous for her heart. The God Who Is would tolerate no future dallying with the gods who were not. When Israel was delivered from Egypt, she had to leave its idols behind. When she crossed the Jordan, God would tolerate no attraction to Canaan's gods either. The first two commandments codified the point, and death was the penalty for disobedience.

> You shall have no other gods before me. You shall not make for yourself an idol in the form of anything in heaven above or on the earth beneath or in the waters below. You shall not bow down to them or worship them; for I [YHWH], your God, am a jealous God . . ." (Exodus 20:3–5).

God himself had exposed the idols of Egypt through the miracles of divine judgment. Then he went ahead of Israel into Canaan, "the hornet" he had promised buzzing the story from mouth to ear along the way (Exodus 23:28; Deuteronomy 7:20; Joshua 24:12). Rahab described what the gossip had done to Jericho's courage: "All who live in this country are melting in fear because of you . . . for the LORD your God is God in heaven above and on the earth below . . ." (Joshua 2:9–11).

God had given Joshua explicit instructions to root out all the idols in Canaan and to destroy all those who worshiped them. His command was not brutal, harsh, or bloodthirsty, but rather loving. Life under the no-gods of Egypt had bitterly enslaved Israel; God did not want his beloved consigned to the tyranny of new ones. At the beginning of the campaign to take the land, Joshua and the people obeyed (Joshua 10:40–42), and when they did, God granted peace and security (11:23). When their faith and zeal wavered and they stopped short of sweeping the leaven of idolatry from the land, the results were disastrous.

Outside In, or Inside Out?

Centuries later, Jesus again sounded the alarm against leaven. He warned his disciples to be on guard against the leaven of the Pharisees, the Sadducees, and Herod (Matthew 16:12; Mark 8:6, 14–15). The leaven of which Jesus spoke was the *teachings* by which these groups enslaved God's people again.

On the surface, his words appear quite straightforward: avoid evil influences like corrupt rulers and bad teachers, and you'll be the better for it. At least that's the usual reading of the text.

Indeed, separating from—even destroying—evil people as protection from their corrupting influence has been a strategy of religious people through the ages. The Pharisees were shocked when Jesus ate with tax collectors and "sinners" (Mark 2:15) because nice Jewish rabbis did not expose themselves, or their followers, to such people. The Jewish cult of the Essenes took separation a step further, withdrawing to the desert of Qumran near the bleak shores of the Dead Sea to avoid the sins of an impure society while creating a new one. Later Christian monastics similarly withdrew from the world to dwell in holy seclusion. One of the strangest of these was Simeon Stylites, who lived from AD 423 to 459 on a six-by-six-foot platform atop a pillar in the Syrian wastelands. The platform was initially fifteen feet high, and Simeon gradually increased its height to achieve a greater degree of separation from the world, until he lived—and died—some sixty feet above the ground. And, of course, in the name of Jesus, the Crusaders slaughtered many Muslim infidels in the eleventh and twelfth centuries, still an issue in Christian witness to the Islamic world today. Perhaps in reaction, Islamic extremists today wage a war of terrorism that is all about purging the leaven of the West from a world they wish to remain pure.

Even in modern churches far removed from the monastic tradition, withdrawal from the culture is a common strategy to avoid corrupting influences and protect the faithful. There are many forms. Some are simple disciplines: avoid those kids at school or the people at work who drink or do drugs, guard what you watch on TV or in the movies, and stay away from bars and loose women. Others are more complex social choices: city dwellers move away from the dangers of the urban core into suburbs and their gated communities; parents pull their children out of public schools and enroll them in private or Christian schools or out of schools altogether, preferring home-schooling.

I understand the logic well; it's all about protection. I used it as a father who wanted desperately to protect my children from what I feared would harm them. I employ it now as a mentor of a fourth-grade student in an urban-core school. Some of the pressures and choices he has to deal with on a daily basis should not be issues a nine- or ten-year-old has to face. Survival requires him to "stay away" from certain people and situations.

But here's the rub: withdrawal doesn't always work. Recently, my hometown newspaper related the front-page story of Jamal, a fourteen-year-old whose mother had hovered over him protectively. Jamal was a good kid, the kind all the neighbors loved. Polite and respectful, he avoided the drugs and gangs that feed on societal peace like cancer does on lung tissue. Jamal died inside his home, inside the protection of his bedroom, a victim of a drive-by shooting. Errant bullets pierced the walls and killed him as he did his homework.

In the same paper, buried on page 3, is another story. This one tells of a gated community whose neighborhood association president was indicted for child molestation.

You can run, but you can't hide. Leaven doesn't only refer to outside influences but describes the power of evil within. Jesus made that clear: "Woe to you, teachers of the law and Pharisees, you hypocrites! You clean the outside of the cup and dish, but inside they are full of greed and self-indulgence. Blind Pharisee! First clean the inside of the cup and dish, and then the outside also will be clean" (Matthew 23:25–26).

The uncomfortable reality is that the dynamic of evil works from the inside out. The human heart doesn't start out as a *tabula rasa*, a tablet clean and pure until external influences corrupt it. The Bible teaches the opposite: we are conceived and born in sin (Psalm 51:5); our hearts are already leavened by evil, and the outflow of sinful behavior in our lives is evidence of the corruption deep within. The prophet Jeremiah calls the heart of man "deceitful . . . and beyond cure" (17:9). The apostle Paul declares "there is no one righteous, not even one" (Romans 3:10).

William Golding's now-classic novel *The Lord of the Flies* was published in Britain in 1954. In the story, British school boys find themselves alone on an island following a plane crash. They begin well, organizing themselves in a proper chain of command as one would expect cultured Brits to do. There are no other people on the island, no negative external influences to corrupt their new world.

Yet the boys soon reveal an evil from within, one already at work in their new society. Fear, cruelty, and violence erupt as desperate struggles for control break their fellowship. The story comes to an uncomfortable head with a particularly grisly murder.

Golding's book sold only three thousand copies in its first years. Both at the time of its publication and now, as a modern classic, it is considered highly controversial.[2] Our age clings desperately to the myth of the basic goodness of man, but Golding's story trades on an unpleasant truth we cannot deny. People that appear cultured, polite, and polished on the outside are driven by ugly impulses, with only a fine line—and sometimes no line at all—separating them from the behavior of the worst of the worst. The best of people—leaders and pastors and teachers and parents—are poisoned by lust that wallpapers their thoughts, greed that consumes their desires, and anger that threatens their relationships.

There's an important corollary to Golding's story: if the dynamic of evil moves not from the outside in but from the inside out, so does the grace of redemption.

Jesus said that a man must be born again to enter the kingdom of God. He meant it. The power of transformation works outwardly from the new heart, giving evidence of new birth within and pressing redemption into the whole of life. A person isn't saved merely because he is exposed to better teaching, follows a superior example, or hangs out with church people and adds religious services to his schedule. A person is *born again* into the kingdom of God; he enters miraculously into a new *kind* of life, one sourced and fueled from heaven by the Spirit of God, one called "eternal life." This life is inseparably linked to the person and work of Jesus himself.

Jesus Cleans House

As Jesus' mere participation in the traditional Seder the night before his death did not exhaust his involvement with the Passover, so his teachings about leaven did not exhaust his involvement with the Feast of Unleavened Bread. His earthly ministry—and especially the passion stories—embodied its customs and traditions.

Jesus celebrated the customary elements of the feast in new and startling ways. As a family head, Jesus oversaw the ceremony of the purging of his house, the ceremony known as *Bedikat HaMetz*. The surprise is

2 It was number 70 on the American Library Association's list of "most challenged" books for the decade of the 1990s.

that the house he cleansed was not merely the room he and his disciples would occupy at the time of the last Passover. Instead, the Gospels tell us that he examined *his royal abode.* In the last days of his earthly life and beginning at the temple in Jerusalem, he searched for leaven in "the house of the Lord."

In the last chapter, I wrote about the extensive examinations of Jesus in his last days, tests that validated that he was the Passover Lamb without blemish. Those tests describe not only an examination *of* Jesus but also an examination *by* Jesus of those who were stewards of Israel. Mark 11 tells the story: Jesus entered Jerusalem triumphantly and went immediately to the temple. He checked it out but retired to Bethany because it was late. On the way back to the temple the next day, he saw a fig tree on the road. Finding only leaves, he cursed the tree because it bore no fruit.

The next morning, the fig tree episode was repeated in an unexpected venue: the temple courts. There, Jesus confronted the buyers, sellers, and money changers, profiteers who did not care about the souls of God's people but only for their own bottom line. In a transparent parallel to the examination of the fig tree, Jesus' search again revealed the same sad reality. There were only leaves—the activities of religion—without the fruit of transformed lives. As in the case of the fig tree, he acted accordingly. He cleansed the temple, driving out the leaven of the buyers and sellers and returning what had become a "den of robbers" to a "house of prayer" (v. 17).

Could the cleansing of the temple actually be *Bedikat HaMetz*? It would seem the connection is at least plausible. The prophet Zephaniah, threatening judgment upon an apostate Jerusalem, points to "the day of the LORD's sacrifice," the death of Messiah. Within the prophet's language lies a reference that seems to point to the festival custom:

> On the day of the LORD's sacrifice, I will punish the princes and the king's sons . . . On that day I will punish all who . . . fill the temple of their gods with violence and deceit . . . *At that time, I will search Jerusalem with lamps* and punish those who are complacent . . ." (Zephaniah 1:8-9, 12, emphasis added).

When Jesus searched the house of the Lord in first-century Jerusalem at the customary time for the ceremony of *Bedikat HaMetz*, he trained his penetrating gaze on the temple of God and discovered the leaven the prophet warned about. He did just what the feast required: he purged his house of its idolatry; he swept the offenders out of the temple; and, knowing full well that they were only the tip of a corrupt iceberg, pointedly challenged their bosses, the chief priests and the teachers of the law who licensed their greedy profit center. "Is it not written: 'My house will be called a house of prayer for all nations'? But you have made it 'a den of robbers' " (Mark 11:17).

Cleaning House Today

Answering the call to search our "house," whether that includes our thought life, our moral behavior, or our families or church fellowships, seems an appropriate way to honor the feast. In so doing, we both pursue holiness and safeguard the freedom of redemption in Christ, a redemption that has a distinctly unleavened characteristic. Jesus will not allow us to minimize the depth of our depravity or deny sin's leavening influence upon our relationships. Instead, he calls us to self-examination of the deepest kind.

Consider this from Jesus' Sermon on the Mount: "I tell you that unless your righteousness surpasses that of the Pharisees and the teachers of the law, you will certainly not enter the kingdom of heaven" (Matthew 5:20). His scalpel cuts deep. There's more to murder than the obvious; anger and self-righteous judgment are evidence of the same sin. His blade flashes again. There's more to adultery than cheating on your wife; the simple game men play—checking out a woman lustfully—is as great a sin, just as surely a corruption of love that is supposed to be pure and faithful and righteous.

Where is Jesus taking us with this unanesthetized soul surgery? His search aims to expose the leaven in our lives. His words are more than "take it or leave it" advice. They reflect his royal right; in his kingdom, leaven has no place. His examination is demanding.

> If your right eye causes you to sin, gouge it out and throw it away. It is better for you to lose one part of your body than for your whole body to be thrown into hell. And if your right hand causes you to sin, cut it off and throw it away. It is better for you to lose one part of your body than for your whole body to go into hell (Matthew 5:29–30).

Though painful, self-examination is crucially important. An incident from my own life illustrates the point.

> The day was December 1, 1997. The doctor's words were chilling. "John, you have leukemia." He paused a few seconds to allow the words to sink in. It didn't take long; I knew the horrible disease intimately. Unbelievably, illogically, contrary to all the statistics, my beloved wife lay dying of the same disease just a few floors above his office. Already ill for almost a full year, she would live only another two months. His next words brought me out of my stunned silence.

"We're going to give you extremely high dose chemotherapy; we'll bring you so close to death that you'll be able to see the edge. The treatment will be hard, even brutal, but that's what it's going to take to save your life."

Statistics were not in my favor, but the choices were slim and none. Chemotherapy began the next day. The first month saw the infusion of a daily cocktail of two chemotherapeutic agents that would cause me to lose my hair on day 11, the callous pads on my palms and the soles of my feet a week or so later, and about forty pounds the first month. At its lowest, my white cell count, written each day on a white board mounted in my room so I could chart daily progress, dropped below 50 (normal is 3,000); my platelets (clotting factor) were less than one percent of what they should have been. The doctor had not lied; I could see death—and even smell it—from my bed.

But progress was real, albeit fragile. The blastocytes in my blood—immature cells produced by cancerous bone marrow—gradually diminished with the chemotherapy's effect.

Acute myeloid leukemia is a cancer of the bone marrow, a systemic disease that is not contained within a solid tumor mass that can be excised or irradiated. To kill the disease, the treatment must also be systemic; every cancerous cell must die. So after a few short weeks of recovery, round 2 began. This involved another month-long course of treatment using two new chemotherapy drugs. These brought more side effects, including nerve damage—thankfully only temporary—that showed up in a daily handwriting exercise in which my signature soon resembled a young child's penmanship. Additional weight loss (sixty-five pounds total) was inevitable since the chemo burned away all the epithelial cells—the surface tissue of my mouth and throat—and I couldn't eat. Chewing and swallowing were impossible; I required feeding through a chest tube for over a month.

But the treatment saved my life. I left the hospital February 25, 1998, and never returned. My wife had left too, almost a month earlier, on January 31, 1998. She had gone to her rest in Christ.

The lesson is straightforward: what is going on inside you is dangerous. Leukemia *can* kill you; but Jesus said that the cancerous leaven of the idolatrous human heart is even more deadly, and *will* kill you.

I tell the story to make an additional point: the cure for leaven, whether cancer or sin, is radical. Chemo was not much fun, but at least its effects could be mitigated with good care and powerful medications. Eliminating the sin from your life by "gouging out your eye" and "cutting off your hand" is not a remedy for the faint of heart, and there are no palliative medicines to make it any easier.

Can This News Be Good?

On first glance, Unleavened Bread seems like anything but a feast. The rigorous self-examination and the ruthless self-denial of which Jesus spoke do not sound much like good news. They sound more like a painful, wearisome, agonizing soul labor that never ends. They bring to mind hair shirts and the self-flagellation of penitents in the Middle Ages, mortifying the flesh for secret sins discovered.

Indeed, the Feast of Unleavened Bread would not celebrate good news except for one thing. *Jesus was buried.*

It happened at dusk, after his body was taken down from the cross by Joseph of Arimathea. He was laid in a new tomb, and the timing of the burial tells the tale. Sundown in first-century Israel signaled the beginning of the new day. That means Jesus was buried not on Passover, but rather as the Feast of Unleavened Bread commenced, specifically fulfilling the requirement: "On the first day remove the yeast from your houses."

The significance of this is momentous. Jesus didn't just *keep* the Feast of Unleavened Bread as a first-century Jew. Jesus *became* the leaven, and his entombment was the cleansing of our lives. It announced that *we* don't sweep our lives clean of the leaven of sin and evil; *he* does. Paul says, "God made him who had no sin to be sin for us, so that in him we might become the righteousness of God" (2 Corinthians 5:21).

In doctrinal terms, as the Passover Lamb, Jesus died as a substitute so that we could be declared *justified* by grace through faith. Jesus was also buried for us as a substitute, taking to the grave with him the leaven of our sin so that we can be declared *sanctified* in him.

Sanctification is an important biblical term, usually understood to be a lifelong process by which the Holy Spirit weans us from sin, a process in which the Scripture calls us to participate by engaging our Spirit-enabled self-discipline. Consider the apostle Paul's words:

> Put to death, therefore, whatever belongs to your earthly nature: sexual immorality, impurity, lust, evil desires, and greed, which is idolatry . . . You used to walk in these ways, in the life you once lived. But now you must rid yourselves of all such things as these: anger, rage, malice, slander, and filthy language from your lips (Colossians 3:5, 7).

But how does one *do* that? How do you actually rid yourself of lust, of evil desires, of greed? I recall reading Benjamin Franklin's program for the "improvement of character." He prescribed that a person should identify one character weakness at a time—laziness or procrastination or impatience—and, focusing upon it with great determination and self-discipline, he would gradually overcome it. Then he could turn to the next flaw. Trouble is, both my ability to diagnosis my "character weaknesses" and the will and self-discipline I would need to root them out are themselves deeply flawed and leavened by sin. People like us don't even know the depth of our sinfulness, much less have the ability to clean up our own act.

Yet behind the call to process-sanctification, behind the insistence on Spirit-empowered self-control, lies an amazing truth: if you have trusted in Christ Jesus, you are *already holy*, already sanctified, for you *were buried with Christ* through your faith in the power of God (Colossians 2:12).

Theologian John Murray gave this reality a name. He called it "definitive sanctification," explaining, "In this matter the indicative lies at the basis of the imperative and our faith of fact is indispensable to the discharge of duty."[3] Murray's language is freighted with grammatical terminology, but his point is pure grace: you are already sanctified because, in faith, you already died and were buried with Christ. That reality becomes the foundation for the new life of obedience that must and will surely follow.

This is helpful, for it sheds light on some passages that don't fit the usual understanding of sanctification. First Corinthians 5:7 is such a passage.

After calling Christ our Passover, Paul moves to the next day and the next feast: "Get rid of the old yeast that you may be a new batch without yeast." Sounds a lot like Franklin's call to personal improvement through the effort of self-discipline, doesn't it? But I stopped too soon; there's more. "Get rid of the old yeast that you may be a new batch without yeast—*as you really are*" (emphasis added). Those who are united to Christ by faith in his death as the Lamb are also united to him in his burial as the leaven. Their sin has been removed, their leaven swept clean, in him.

That's the point of the ethical challenge in Romans 6:2–3, 11. In the first of these verses, Paul reminds us, "We died to sin; how can we live

3 John Murray, *Redemption Accomplished and Applied*, Grand Rapids: Wm. B. Eerdmans Publishing Co., 1955), 146.

in it any longer?" Then joining the two dimensions of sanctification into one, he affirms both the indicative and the imperative: we are definitively cleansed in Christ, and we ought to live like it practically. Verse 11 adds the punch: "In the same way, *count yourselves dead to sin* but alive to God in Christ Jesus" (emphasis added). The apostle here uses a word that suggests a careful and intentional thought process. In essence, here's how the logic works: you're dead to sin, for you died with Christ. What's more, you're already buried with him, removing the leaven of sin from you once and for all. You're clean. Now, *go live like it!*

The Feast of Unleavened Bread proclaimed a crucial component of the good news of God, but it pointed forward toward Messiah and a dimension of redemption never before known. Old Testament Israel had to be reminded—by the annual removal of leaven—that she was free from Egypt. The Feast gave the Israelites a taste of good news, but it was short lived and easily forgotten because it was only a shadow of the lasting freedom that would prove so elusive, the freedom from the power of evil within. Even when God gave her the new land of Canaan, requiring only that she sweep the land clean of its idols and those that worshiped them, Israel fell short. The sad summary is sounded in Judges 1:28: "When Israel became strong, they pressed the Canaanites into forced labor, but never drove them out completely." Because leaven remained within the land, Israel was never really free. Because of her failure, God announced, "I will not drive them out before you; they will be thorns in your sides and their gods will be a snare to you" (Judges 2:3). Israel wept aloud.

The reality of sanctification would not come by a people's effort, even if led by priests and prophets and hounded by their own conscience. It would be found only in Christ Jesus. Paul said it simply: it is Christ Jesus who "is our righteousness, holiness and redemption" (1 Corinthians 1:30).

This is radical news—riotous news—for it is *already* true, even though we have *not yet* been able to put away all of sin's leaven this side of the grave. Even if the addictive characteristics of alcoholism plague you every day, even if a bad temper makes you ashamed and your family afraid, even if you struggle with the destructive sin of gossip despite promising yourself and God that you will stop, you are holy if you truly trust in Christ.

Some may think I've gone too far. "You've killed the call to obedience. You've gutted the importance of repentance and silenced the call to turn away from sin. You've embraced licentiousness and waved off Jesus' call to self-denial. You've destroyed the very doctrine of sanctification you claim to be teaching!"

No, I have not. All of the doctrines just mentioned refer to important biblical realities, each of them crucial to the life of faith. But neither the quality of our repenting nor the quality of our obeying *determines* our holiness. Instead, like a stream that flows from its headwaters to spread new life across the barren desert, repentance and obedience flow into our lives only from the holiness that already belongs to us in Christ—*by grace through faith*.[4]

The new life that would cause the desert to bloom would show its first flower the very next day.

Questions for Further Study and Discussion

1. Since Jesus' burial was an activity of gracious redemption, it thus should inspire our grateful worship similarly to the way the cross and resurrection do. Why do you suppose there are so many Good Friday and Easter hymns, but none that sing of Jesus' burial? Exercise your creative side: try writing a verse to fit an existing song that would celebrate the truth of the burial of Christ.
2. Explain the tension between the burial of Jesus as the definitive cleansing of the people of God and the many passages that instruct us to put off the works of sin and put on those of faith.
3. When you study the Christian church today (including *your* church), do you see fruit or only leaves? What should be done about it?
4. A friend of mine and his spouse devote the last week of each year to prayerful self- examination. Together they examine the state of their family's life. They look at physical health, discussing diet, exercise, and concerns they have for each other as they advance in years. They talk about financial health and stewardship. They examine evidences of faith in their own lives and in their children's. They talk about the health of their marriage. The annual practice has changed the way they live, adding a vigorous sense of purpose where they once were driven by happenstance. Allow me to suggest that you initiate a similar conversation with those closest to you in the family of faith. If you do, share some of your insights with your study group or accountability partner.

4 For a wonderful explanation of this, see Bryan Chapell, *Holiness by Grace: Delighting in the Joy That Is Our Strength* (Wheaton, IL: Crossway Books, 2001).

Chapter 4

AWAKE THE DAWN!

THE FEAST OF FIRSTFRUITS

Leviticus 23:9–14

I was watching my grandsons—at that time seven and nine years old—open Christmas gifts. It was, frankly, an exercise in barely restrained violence. Each gift, so carefully and lovingly wrapped by mother, aunt, or grandma, was torn free from its colorful paper and ribbon in mere seconds, with no concern at all for saving the wrapping paper. (My mother would be appalled.) With their wide eyes and smiles to match, the boys offered genuine but hurried "thank yous" that barely escaped their lips before the magnetic pull of the next gift overwhelmed their senses, and they were drawn by internal forces to rip it open too.

The children of Israel opened the festal gifts of God with the same frenzied pace. The Feast of Passover was celebrated on the fourteenth of Nisan. The fifteenth brought the Feast of Unleavened Bread. Left breathless from the ceremonies, their bellies stretched because of the rich food, their hearts and minds swimming with rich truths, the Israelites were still reveling in the shadows of redemption and hope that these first two festivals cast when—almost before they knew it—the next festival on the sixteenth of Nisan was upon them. It was called Firstfruits, the third of the spring feasts.

The Requirements of the Feast

Firstfruits was never celebrated in Egypt or even on the sojourn Israel made through the wilderness. It would not have made sense; in the wilderness, Israel was nomadic; she neither planted nor harvested, so there were no firstfruits to gather. Instead, she lived by sheer grace in God's provision of manna, water, and quail. Firstfruits would not commence until Israel entered the land of Canaan and the manna ceased, replaced with the routine—but still gracious—gifts of his love that grew bountifully in the land of milk and honey.

As with both Passover and Unleavened Bread, this feast had both personal and communal dimensions, much like holidays today. Thanksgiving gatherings in the United States, for example, are usually family-based festivities, complete with a meal fit for royalty. Turkey, ham, roast, or prime rib graces the holiday tables of most people. One family I know uses this national holiday as the basis for an extended family reunion. With crowds exceeding a hundred, their family affair is larger than many churches. Others wrap their celebration around the national pastime of professional football, either loving or loathing the Dallas Cowboys or the Detroit Lions and their opponent of the day. Many other Christians wouldn't think of celebrating Thanksgiving without going to church. For them, Thanksgiving is no mere national holiday; it is a time for communal worship and prayer.

Like Thanksgiving Day in the United States, Firstfruits celebrations in ancient Israel varied from family to family. Some families perhaps gathered at the grandparents' home; others at the oldest son's. Some had large families and likely experienced the family drama well known to many even today. Others were smaller gatherings, more intimate and sedate. But every celebration was to be shaped by the character of the feast as a rehearsal of redemption. Deliverance from Egypt by the blood of the lamb had accomplished a fresh start, and Unleavened Bread had punctuated the break with the past. Those rehearsals of redemption would tilt Israel forward to new life; it was a life that would find its type in the firstfruits of the new land, one that would always long for more.

A Harvest Feast

The feast fit naturally into the agrarian calendar of the Middle East, its prescriptions timed to the bounty of the harvest blessings in the land God had given his people. Yet Passover had reset her calendar so that her new life was defined by redemption, not agriculture. Appropriately, the feast was tabernacle-based at first, the festivities moving to the temple after Solomon's magnificent structure was finished.

In Israel's earliest days in the land of Canaan, the festival was very simple. As the spring rains nourished the fields and the Mediterranean sun warmed the crops, the barley and flax began to show the first signs of ripening in what had formerly been the seventh month of the agricultural calendar. As the fields, until now a sea of deep green, began to show the first waves of gold, an Israelite farmer would gather an early ripening sheaf of his barley harvest and bring it to the priest. He, in turn, waved it before the LORD on the day after the Sabbath, a token of gratitude and praise for God's gracious gift. This wave offering was accompanied by another burnt offering, a year-old lamb without defect, as well as a grain offering, 4.5 liters of fine flour mixed with oil, and a drink offering of a quart of wine.[1]

In praise for the wonderful grace of God, Deuteronomy 26:11 describes what happened next. Simply put, Israel had a party! The people and the Levites and even the aliens among them "[rejoiced] in all the good things" God had given. They ate until they were full, feasting with glad and thankful hearts.

With the passing centuries, the customs of this feast became more structured, particularly those of the communal celebration based in the temple. Alfred Edersheim suggests that by the first century, an elaborate ceremony would develop to "launch" the harvest with pomp and circumstance. The Sanhedrin, or ruling council of Israel, having determined some days before the exact plot of land from which the sheaf was to be cut, sent three men to that plot, each with a sickle and a basket, just before the sun went down on the fifteenth of Nisan.

> "[T]hey first asked of the bystanders three times each of these questions: 'Has the sun gone down?' 'With this sickle?' 'Into this basket?'
> 'On this Sabbath . . . ?'—and, lastly, 'Shall I reap?' Having each time been answered in the affirmative, they cut down barley to the amount

1 Tremper Longman III provides a helpful explanation of these offerings: "The *'olah* (burnt offering) emphasized the atonement nature of sacrifice, while the *minhah* (grain offering and wine) highlighted that the offering was a gift." Yet it was a gift with a sense of duty: it was tribute paid to the king. *Immanuel in Our Place: Seeing Christ in Israel's Worship* (Phillipsburg, NJ: P & R Publishing, 2001), 77– 92.

of one ephah, or ten omers, or three seahs, which is equal to about three pecks and three pints of our English measure."[2]

Tilting Forward

Both the developing traditions and the involvement of the Sanhedrin and the priesthood in the temple serve to indicate that Firstfruits was more than just a thanksgiving celebration. While Israel was indeed grateful for the bountiful harvest that had been growing in the field for months, Firstfruits had a spiritual significance. Israel brought sheaves of *new* grain, a gift that carried within it signs of hope for a *new life.*

This forward-leaning approach to the harvest festival required faith, a way of viewing life that needed the heart—and not just the eyes—to see. It served in stark contrast to the fear-based superstition of the nations around them. The Baal worshipers in Canaan negotiated with their gods desperately, seeking to persuade and cajole by cutting themselves until they bled (as did the Baal priests on Mount Carmel) or burning their children in the flames to secure prosperity (as the horrible Molech cult did). Each year, religious success would be calibrated in bushels per acre and religious failure in deaths per family.

Israel didn't have to negotiate with God to care for her daily and annual needs; he had promised to do so in love. On a daily basis, she would gratefully acknowledge his bounty, give thanks to the LORD, and enjoy life in fellowship with him. Yet even in the land of milk and honey, all was not yet right, as those with a tender heart could see. Many among her were enslaved, dependent, and impoverished by the circumstances of life. The alien, the fatherless, and the widow who lived in Israel were not only poor but defenseless, vulnerable to abuse by the unscrupulous. God had already revealed his own character; he would surely rise to their defense (Deuteronomy 10:17–18). He expected his people to do the same.

To give structure and visibility to this mercy mandate, God worked several practices into the fabric of Israel's communal life, practices that reflected the theme of the Feast of Firstfruits. Deuteronomy 24:17–22 established laws that governed *gleaning*, a practice central to the narrative in the book of Ruth. Landowners like Boaz were intentionally to leave the corners of their fields unharvested, allowing the poor—like Naomi and Ruth—to gather food in order to survive

2 Alfred Edersheim, *The Temple, Its Ministry and Services as They Were at the Time of Christ* (Garland, TX: Galaxie Software, 2000), electronic edition.

And Deuteronomy 26 linked Firstfruits with another form of the same spirit of mercy, the *tithe*, a tenth of all the bounty with which God had blessed her, to be given to the priest in the temple.

Whether Firstfruits was a form of the tithe, or the tithe and gleaning were forms of Firstfruits, it seems clear that the three were all expressions of the same heart of faith. Giving a portion back to God was intended to put legs and feet under Israel's desire for mercy and justice. All three were to be joyous gifts that told of the squinting vision of faith, gifts that gave expression to the longing of the soul for a new life where love for God and others would replace self-interest as the way of living.

Over time, however, the mercy mandate was forgotten, and the giving practices God had required of Israel lost their meaning. Israel's tithes reflected her heart: as it grew cold, she presented her tithe mechanically at best and resentfully most other times. Often she did not give at all. The prophet Malachi exposed the ugliness of Israel's heart by pointing out the empty temple storehouses. Her failure to give "[oppressed] the widows and the fatherless, deprived the aliens of justice" and robbed God of his due (Malachi 3:5). And when Israel's spiritual leaders did ramp up the pressure to give, all became fixated on *how* more than on *why*. Thus, the conservative Pharisees of the first century faithfully gave a tithe even of their herbs and spices—their "mint, dill and cumin"—but hypocritically neglected the more important matters of the law—justice, mercy and faithfulness" (Matthew 23:23).

Sadly, many believers in Christ today have lost this sense of the tithe as *rehearsal*, of giving mercy with a forward-tilt. Many think tithing is the divinely prescribed method to determine the required percentage to give to church and charitable causes. Worse, many in the United States have been seduced into thinking that giving God his 10 percent will assure his blessing on their 90 percent. (I saw a bumper sticker the other day that said it better than I can: "If 10% is enough for God, it should be enough for the IRS.") Evangelical pulpits sound forth a gospel of wealth, and charities across the land play into it, suggesting (implicitly if not explicitly) that giving is a way of getting rich. The tax code aggravates the problem: giving in many churches is substantially higher in December than it is in January. The IRS tax benefits for charitable contributions and the lure for many of having a building named for them tend to feed the very self-interest that the tithe existed to correct.[3]

Motive is not the only problem with our giving. The wealth we keep can also be dangerous. Wealth is not inherently evil, of course. It is, properly understood, an extravagant gift of God's grace that enables people both to enjoy God's good creation and to show generosity in a way that reflects a longing for righteousness to flow to all.[4] Yet wealth can infect the heart. If it is shaped by self-interest, money becomes power and erupts in ugly displays of oppression.

In a sin-twisted world, where governments and economies have long served the power of evil, God is at work redeeming. He has always cared deeply about the effects of sin's brokenness upon his whole creation. The network of benevolence he established—beginning with Firstfruits but including the tithe and the gleaning customs—was a taste, back in the kitchen, of the bounteous life that was yet to come. And he wanted his people to hunger for it.

Firstfruits and Redemption

Like the other feasts, Firstfruits is a type (*tupos*) of the fuller redemption that would come in Christ. Once more, the timing tells the story. Remember the calendar: Passover was the fourteenth of Nisan, and Unleavened Bread was the fifteenth. Christ was offered up as the Passover lamb on the former, and he was buried on the eve of the latter. The evening and the day of the next day—the sixteenth of Nisan—began the Feast of Firstfruits. This is the day we call Easter, the day Jesus rose from the grave.

The timing of the resurrection of Jesus was no accident. It didn't just happen to occur on a nice but incidental Jewish feast day (similar to the way that my birthday occurs on the same date as the Food and Wine Festival in Charleston, South Carolina—nice, but irrelevant). No, the resurrection of Jesus the Messiah finds its meaning in the fact that God planned it according to the festal calendar of Israel. God structured

3 Despite such benefits, Christian giving is nowhere near 10 percent of income; it is not even substantially above the national average of charitable giving of 2.3 percent. *Annual Report on Philanthropy for the Year 2004* (Indianapolis: Giving USA Foundation; AAFRC Trust for Philanthropy, Center of Philanthropy at Indiana University, 2005).

4 John R. Schneider extols a right view of wealth in *The Good of Affluence: Seeking God in a Culture of Wealth* (Grand Rapids: William B. Eerdmans Publishing Co., 2002).

redemption not only so that Jesus would be in the grave until the third day (as required by the "sign of Jonah" in Matthew 12:39–41), but especially so that Jesus would break open the grave *on the Feast of Firstfruits*. That feast thus defines the meaning of the resurrection: it was not merely the miracle of life after death but *the dawning of a new world after the death of the old.*

The Bible explains just how and why this is good news.

Firstfruits of the Grave

First, Jesus' resurrection was the firstfruits of the physical grave. With compelling logic, the apostle Paul reflects on the resurrection of Christ, concluding: "If Christ has not been raised, your faith is futile; you are still in your sins . . . but Christ has indeed been raised from the dead, the *firstfruits* of those who have fallen asleep" (1 Corinthians 15:17, 20, emphasis added). This is amazing news for all who live in the frailty of mortal flesh. Death has long marked our life and our world, and all of us one day will face our own physical end. Worse, on the way to the grave we will grieve real tears over loved ones whom death will snatch away from us. Death hurts! And if death is the final result of following God, faith is a waste of time.

But, says Paul, *it is not the end.* Death once was the judicial result of sin (Genesis 2:17; 1 Corinthians 15:56), but in Christ, sin has been overcome—and death with it. Thus Paul can exultantly cry, "Death has been swallowed up in victory!" (15:54).

The resurrection of Christ was the firstfruits of the resurrection of the body. It waved the first sheaves of physical new life, opening a way beyond death for those who die in the Lord. An even fuller harvest will come with the opening of their graves. The church throughout the ages has confessed such a longing in the Apostle's Creed: "I believe in the resurrection of the body."

> Gretchen had ALS—Lou Gehrig's disease. The disease is terrible, its process glacial in pace. Gretchen died by inches, an interminable eighteen months from diagnosis to life's end. From an active and vibrant life, she was slowly but inexorably reduced first to pain, then to a walker, then to a wheelchair. Subsequent limitations brought the loss of speech, then the loss of mobility, and, finally, the loss of dignity. Finally confined to her bed, she was stripped of every sign of life except for her exquisite consciousness: cruelly, she was fully aware of everything. Through it all, her husband Lee loved her well, caring for her with a tenderness that was a model of love.

Her death brought a strange mixture of emotions to the community of faith. We smiled and laughed as we remembered her life the way she had lived it, always filled with joy. We grieved and lamented her life as it had ended: she so frail, and we so impotent to stop the horrid progress of the disease.

At her funeral, we processed our grief with tears while holding tight to the hope of our faith. Confessing the Creed with both vigor and volume, we declared our belief in "the resurrection of the body, and the life everlasting." And, it seemed, just beyond the audible sound of our voices in north Texas, a chorus of faint voices echoed back. They were the voices of Grandpa and Grandma, of Calvin and Luther, of Augustine and Anselm, of Paul and Peter—of all for whom the resurrection of Christ was the surety of another resurrection.

When at last the memorial service ended, many remained at the cemetery for a long time, hugging, weeping, laughing, and sharing grief together.

We stood around the open grave so much longer than customary that the funeral director approached Lee quietly, wondering whether he might lower the casket into the ground, adding almost apologetically, "You can stay if you'd like to watch." The mourners looked shocked at the prospect of watching the lowering of the casket into a hole in the ground. American funeral customs have changed; the stark reality of that hole doesn't seem to fit with the fake green grass that hides the pile of dirt or with the silk-lined and furniture-grade wood casket that looks almost comfy, hermetically-sealed in a pathetic attempt to prevent the decay that will inevitably intrude.

But Lee wasn't concerned about changing funeral customs; he was gripped by faith. He didn't blink before answering the mortician's question with a quiet but firm, "Yes, we'll stay." The silent crowd converged upon the perfect rectangle, watching in silence as Gretchen's body was lowered into the ground. A few handfuls of dirt broke the silence with a percussive beat on the casket lid. Lee cleared his throat, wiped his tears, put an arm around me, and said in an unwavering voice loud enough for everyone present to hear, "Let's go get some coffee."

One lady gasped at what I'm sure she took for insensitivity. I was moved to tears. Lee wasn't coldhearted; his words were, simply, a profession of faith. Lee believed in the resurrection of the dead.

He really believed that death was not the end for his bride, nor would it be for him.

For Jesus the Messiah was raised from the dead as firstfruits.

Firstfruits of a New World

Jesus' resurrection was the dawn of something bigger than life after physical death. According to 1 Corinthians 15:45, Jesus was the "last Adam." His cross had marked the death of the first Adam's world, one that had been held in the grip of death ever since the fall into sin. His resurrection was thus the dawn of a new world, a new heaven and earth. Paul explains: The first creation had been "subjected to frustration, not by its own choice, but by the will of the one who subjected it"; and the results of the first Adam's sin had been cosmic—"the whole creation has been groaning . . ." But the death and resurrection of the last Adam brought hope to creation itself. The old world frustrations that plagued the land with weeds, streams and air with pollution, and cells with ALS or cancer, are nearing an end. "The creation itself will be liberated from its bondage to decay and brought into the glorious freedom of the children of God" (Romans 8:18–21).

When will that world appear? Most assume it will be at some indefinite future, at the time of Jesus' return. But Christ's resurrection on Firstfruits means the new world *has dawned.* Paul boldly declares in Romans 8:23, that we already "have the firstfruits of the Spirit" as evidence of the fact.[5] Make no mistake, the new creation is not yet fully revealed; believers themselves groan for the completion of redemption, for more is yet to come. But dawn has surely broken.

In Scripture, this new world is a kingdom, a reign of grace that will one day bring healing to the whole of God's cosmos. This new world order is called by various terms in the Bible. Jesus called it "the kingdom of God" (Mark 1:15) and "the kingdom of heaven" (Matthew 4:17). John's gospel refers to it as a new kind of life called "eternal life" (3:16). In Revelation 21:1, it is simply called "a new heaven and a new earth." The surprise in this last passage is that the new heaven and new earth is not exclusively future but makes its appearance here and now. It takes faith to see it, of course; each day we are confronted with the evil and brokenness so evident in our world. Yet the new world *is* opening up.

Medical science has learned much about cancer and how to fight it. It speaks almost reverentially about macrophages. A macrophage is a

5 Richard B. Gaffin, Jr., *Resurrection and Redemption: A Study in Paul's Soteriology* (Phillipsburg, NJ: P&R Publishing, 1987), 41ff.

marvelous type of white blood cell that destroys invading cells, even cancerous ones. The name means "big eater" and defines its function; a macrophage devours malignant cells, even consuming the debris left behind after the enemy is destroyed. But a macrophage doesn't only attack the problem; it then beefs up the solution, stimulating a growing colony of new cells that boosts the body's immune system, thus feeding the healthy new life it leaves in its wake.

The power of Jesus' resurrection as firstfruits works similarly. On the cross, he devoured sin; rising from the grave, he conquered death. But he didn't stop there. His resurrection was but the beginning of a bigger harvest. The gospel of the risen Christ is literally producing colonies of new life that are spreading over the globe. Believers are, to use N. T. Wright's lovely metaphor, "citizens of heaven, colonizing the earth."[6]

These colonies are evidence that the new heaven and the new earth is breaking in to this world. It is very real, is clearly identified in Scripture, and is given a name. John, in the Bible's next to last chapter, uses three metaphors to describe it: he calls it "the new Jerusalem," "the bride beautifully dressed for her husband," and "the wife of the Lamb." All three are biblical metaphors, not for heaven, but for the *church*. John is not describing the church after the Lord returns but rather is talking about the church *now*, a community of faith described as God sees her through the spectacles of Messiah: dead to sins because of the cross, made holy because of his burial, and raised to new life by his resurrection.

You might have to think about this for a while. Most who read the Bible's last book assume that it talks about an exclusively future hope. Likewise, most who know the church of the Lord intimately would hardly describe it as heaven on earth.

Yet Paul affirms this clearly (don't miss the verb tenses): "If anyone is in Christ, he *is* a new creation; the old *has gone*, the new *has come*!" (2 Corinthians 5:17, emphasis added). "When he speaks here of 'new creation,' this is not meant merely in an individual sense ('a new creature'), but one is to think of the new world of the re-creation that God has made to dawn in Christ, and in which everyone who is in Christ is included."[7]

6 N. T. Wright, *Surprised by Hope: Rethinking Heaven, the Resurrection, and the Mission of the Church* (New York: HarperOne, 2008), 100.

7 Herman Ridderbos, *Paul: An Outline of His Theology* (Grand Rapids: William B. Eerdmans Publishing Co., 1975), 45.

Firstfruits People

Believers in Christ are Firstfruits people, not just people who expect to go to heaven when they die. Their lives already produce a different harvest. They are compelled by new- world impulses; they are different *within*. No longer are they marked by only the anger, malice, violence, greed, lust, and selfishness that are the normal harvest of the flesh.[8] Instead, their lives reveal the beginnings of authentic change: "The fruit of the Spirit is love, joy, peace, patience, kindness, goodness, faithfulness, gentleness and self-control . . . Those who belong to Christ Jesus have crucified the sinful nature with its passions and desires" (Galatians 5:22–24).

More is yet to come. What dawned in Christ's resurrection and has begun to bear fruit in us will one day renew *all things* in a harvest bounty beyond all comprehension. Paul bubbled over when he thought of it:

> No eye has seen,
>   no ear has heard,
> no mind has conceived
> what God has prepared for those who love him—but God has revealed it
>   to us by his Spirit (1 Corinthians 2:9–10).

The full harvest will bring sweet reconciliation through Christ to every dimension of life (Colossians 1:20). I'll talk more about that in the last chapter, but I invite you to reflect for just a moment how much fits into the phrase "all things." Redemption this comprehensive will bring healing to marriages you might think are beyond hope, peace between nations that have torn at each other's throats for centuries, shalom to city streets long bloodied by violence and colored by fear, and healing to bodies racked with pain and dying from disease. The creation groaning under pesticides, pollution, and the rape of the land will finally find rest.

Redemption that touches "all things" will be redemption grand in scope indeed!

Firstfruits of Our Witness

Recall that there were two sides to the coin of the Old Testament Feast

---

8 The Greek word for flesh, *sarx*, has several distinct shades of meaning that range from physical bodies to the spiritual force that is the counterpart to "the Spirit." Gerhard Kittel and Gerhard Friedrich, eds., *Theological Dictionary of the New Testament*, trans. by Geoffrey W. Bromiley (Grand Rapids: Eerdman's Publishing, 1985), 1004–5.

of Firstfruits. First, it was a celebration of thanks. After the ceremonies marking the day, the presentation of the sheaf of grain, and the waving of the *'omer*, God's people lustily enjoyed the fruit of God's redemption with a literal feast in the land of milk and honey. The other side of the coin showed a dark side of the Feast. In the shadow of the party, gleaning laws and the tithe regulations reminded Israel that everything—this side of glory—was not yet right. She was to hunger for more, leaning forward toward a new day, acknowledging with her generous gifts of mercy the needs of the dependent, the needy, and the defenseless.

The resurrection of Jesus the Christ on the sixteenth of Nisan also sounds this two-note chord. On the one hand, Christ's resurrection allows believers to experience, and thus to see and celebrate already, the gracious gifts of the Holy Spirit. The Spirit is a "deposit guaranteeing our inheritance" (Ephesians 1:14), allowing us to rest assured in the comfort of God's promises. On the other, the resurrection of Christ anticipates a fuller harvest of redemption. Believers can't help but see all around them that life has a long way to go before God completes his redeeming work.

Just here, in the middle of this tension, God has a surprise for us: we have a role in bringing that harvest of new life.

Jesus told us how new life would be planted and how it would ripen. The parable of the sower explained that the Word of God would be sown like a tiny seed, yet would produce "a hundred, sixty or thirty times what was sown" (Matthew 13:8). The Feast of Firstfruits would embody the lesson: *each believer* bears that seed in his new life of faith, for the church of the risen Christ is made up of people living life on a mission. Having themselves been changed by grace, they now carry the Word with them, planting the seed of the gospel here and there. How? Colossians 4:5 gives us a picture: "Be wise in the way you act toward outsiders; make the most of every opportunity. Let your conversation be always full of grace, seasoned with salt." The last allusion refers to the ancient practice of sealing covenants not with a signature but with the exchange of salt, thereby signifying permanence and preservation. God wants our conversations to have eternal consequences. That takes gospel intentionality, whether at a neighborhood coffee shop, in a mentoring relationship with a youngster, or on a cell phone chat with an old friend.

We don't save anyone, of course. Yet God wants us to know the significance of our personal faith in this harvest of new life and thus to be encouraged in our witness. Two overlooked passages make this point. In the first, Paul mentions that Epenetus "was the *first convert* to Christ in the province of Asia" (Romans 16:5, emphasis added). A second, similar to it, appears in 1 Corinthians 16:15. "You know that the household of Stephanas were the *first converts* in Achaia" (emphasis added). Why would Paul make specific reference to individuals in early church history who, by almost anyone's reckoning, were incidental to the main flow of the story? Was he a detail freak, anxious to make sure that accurate records were kept? Not a chance. Paul was a first-rate rabbinic scholar, and he knew full well the significance of the principle of firstfruits. He was telling the early church—and us two thousand years later—that as the new world dawned in the resurrection of Christ, so the fuller harvest of the new heaven and new earth spreads to one person at a time through believers' networks of relationships and spheres of influence. Epenetus and Stephanas, first in their region to believe in Christ, were but first sheaves of harvest grain. The greater harvest will come through the work of the gospel borne by servants like them.

The harvest is God's alone. A seed that becomes a plant that bears fruit reflects mysterious natural forces. So does a Word that generates faith that bears a spiritual harvest. The power for this harvest comes alone from the Spirit of God.

That power is the focus of the next feast.

Questions for Further Study and Discussion

1. How is the New Testament Feast of Firstfruits (Jesus' resurrection) a harvest festival?
2. There were two earthquakes recorded at the end of Matthew's telling of the gospel. One (27:51) is mentioned as occurring at the moment of Jesus' death. The other (28:2) is the "violent earthquake" that accompanies the opening of Christ's tomb. Why are these important?
3. The chapter makes the claim that the resurrection of Christ is the dawn of a new creation and that believers are the firstfruits of that world: "If anyone is in Christ, he is a new creation" (2 Corinthians 5:17). Meditate on that for a while. What evidence of that new world do you see in the lives of Christians you know? In your own life?
4. Discuss funeral practices in your church and community. Do those practices adequately "tilt people forward" toward a future resurrection of the body, or do they exclusively focus on remembering the life just ended? How would you suggest they be improved to give clearer testimony to our faith?
5. Do you tithe? If so, compare your motives with those Paul mentions in 2 Corinthians 9:6–15.

Chapter 5

POWER TO THE PEOPLE!

THE FEAST OF PENTECOST

Leviticus 23:15–22; Acts 2

JD was still married when I met him, but the marriage was on life support. The problem was simple: JD was an adulterer. He laid the blame for his sin on sexual patterns begun long before, patterns modeled by a father who intentionally exposed his son to pornography and prostitution as coming-of-age rituals. By the time I met him, he had frequented brothels in many cities and run up thousands of dollars of debt on a secret credit card designated solely for his illicit hobby. And he had just got caught by his wife.

JD wanted help. He was hoping I would help him establish boundaries that would keep him from trouble. He wanted me to tell him that he could go out with the guys only once a week, and then only if a church friend was in attendance. He wanted me to tell him TGI Friday's was okay, but Hooters was off limits. But JD had lived with rules like that for nearly eight years of marriage, and it hadn't worked.

As his secrets were exposed like an onion being peeled—one stinking layer at a time—his wife became involved in the game, shifting into the role of private detective, a traffic cop, the heavy, the Enforcer. Thinking these roles were her responsibility, she played at the game with zeal.

JD was better at the game. While his wife checked credit card statements to look for illicit purchases, he signed up for new cards with a different billing address. When she scoured the home computer to check on his Internet usage, he bought a small laptop he could use anywhere. When she began to check up on him at work and the health club to verify that he was where he said he'd be, he simply took his habit on the road, trolling for illicit lovers when he traveled for business.

He got caught again, this time by a microscopic bug. He brought a venereal disease home to his wife.

JD was more ashamed and even more desperate. Accountability to rules hadn't worked. Perhaps he should get more serious about his religion.

Which books should he read? Which Sunday school class should he take? Which men's group would help him save his marriage?

But religious disciplines would prove futile, too. JD didn't need laws or religion; he needed power, power of the kind that would change him within. It is the power God's people had always needed, a power about which he taught her in the Feast of Weeks.

Let's start this chapter with a bit of a review. All of the festivals God established were intended to call his Old Testament people to celebrate, to remember the blessings that he had already given but also to yearn in faith, to anticipate the fuller redemption Messiah would bring. Thus, each of the festivals served as a type or shadow, an actual but early taste of that redemption to come. Further, the festivals were structured around the rhythm of the Sabbath, because all—without exception—were designed to encourage Israel to long for rest. The Sabbath rhythm pulsed through all seven feasts—a full "week" of feasts—to give shape to this longing.

The first three feasts—the spring festivals of Passover, Unleavened Bread, and Firstfruits—were foundational because of the events they celebrated. Passover was the bedrock: Israel was to learn that her life was founded on grace, for she was redeemed by the blood of another. Unleavened Bread taught her that delivered people were a holy people, free not only in name but truly unleavened from the enslaving power of sin and idolatry and called to live that way. And God had set his people free for a purpose: to live as the presence of the future, early evidence of the new world he was bringing.

We have also seen that these three foundational feasts link to Christ's earthly ministry. He died on Passover as the atoning sacrifice for our sins, as our justification. He was buried on Unleavened Bread as our sanctification, putting a gracious end to sin's control. And he was raised on Firstfruits, his own resurrected body serving as the first sheaf of grain of the new creation to come.

Israel would pause for seven weeks and a day before she could celebrate again in the next festival of the divine sequence. The wait would be worth it; the next feast portrayed an expansion of redemption that went beyond anything she could imagine.

History of the Feast

The Feast of Weeks was a harvest festival, one that brought to a conclusion a celebration that had begun with Firstfruits. The two were as inseparably connected to each other as Unleavened Bread was to Passover. Because of this connection, it was celebrated only after Israel entered the land and began to enjoy its rich bounty.

The feasting actually began as Israel took seriously the instruction to "count" the days after Firstfruits (Leviticus 23:15–16). The countdown, or "counting the *'omer*," tracked carefully the seven full weeks. Each evening, the family head would mark off the day just ended in some creative way that would teach the children the promise and the expectation of the harvest hope. In time, Psalm 67 became a favorite. It was often recited each day, its seven verses and forty-nine words (in Hebrew) adding a symbolism beyond its harvest theme. Its confident conclusion reminded Israel that her life had a purpose beyond herself: "God will bless us, and all the ends of the earth will fear him" (v. 7).

After the counting and the waiting, the feast day finally came at the end of the wheat harvest. Again, the day was a *miqra qodes,* a sacred assembly for the entire community to rejoice in the good gifts of God's bounty and to rehearse what was to come. Israel offered up tokens of the harvest goodness of the land in a time of worship that took on the character of a thanksgiving celebration. The grain offering was new grain, kneaded into two loaves made *with* yeast, a sign of the goodness of the new land of "milk and honey" and a harbinger of the new world to come when sin would corrupt nothing.[1] The loaves were accompanied by burnt offerings to the LORD, the sweet smell of the smoke rising to heaven simply to tickle God's nostrils with the fragrance of pure worship and praise. Sin offerings, required on behalf of the priest, involved a goat and two lambs.

In the description of the regulations for the feast, God established gleaning laws that would add an element of mercy to the festal celebration (Leviticus 23:22), echoing the same practice in Firstfruits. The God of the fatherless, the widow, and the alien would not overlook such defenseless ones in the bounty of his grace.

No passages in the Torah linked the Feast of Weeks to a single redemptive event the way that Passover had been connected to the exodus. God's provision of a rich land of milk and honey after over four centuries of bondage and forty years of wandering in the desert was a sufficient reason to feast. Israel might simply have viewed the Feast of Weeks the way Americans think of Thanksgiving Day, a pause in the routine to celebrate God's blessings in general. Yet, as the years in Canaan passed, the traditions surrounding this feast revealed God's deeper purposes for it. By the time of the late Old Testament period, two noteworthy developments had occurred: first, the feast was no longer called Weeks but Pentecost; second, and more significantly, the feast had become formally linked by the rabbinic tradition to the giving of the law at Sinai.

The dating of Israel's arrival at Sinai (Exodus 19:1) seems to fit. Fifty days after departing Egypt, Israel indeed found herself at the foot of that mountain. She had been delivered by the mighty hand and outstretched arm of YHWH, had witnessed the total devastation of Pharaoh and his army, had walked through the sea on dry ground, and had been gathered to him at the base of the mountain from which he would establish his covenant. He would be their God, and they would be his special people, redeemed for his own possession.

---

1 Differences of opinion exist on the significance of the bread containing leaven. Noordtzij (*Leviticus,* 236) finds in it a reference to Israel's normal fare, and thus views the offering as thanksgiving for *daily* bread. Hartley (op. cit.) sees the leaven simply as a symbol of a "joyous occasion." Edward Chumney, *The Seven Festivals of the Messiah* (Shippensburg, PA: Treasure House, 1994), 94, thinks leaven here suggests that Israel's national existence included within it sinful people. Leavened bread in this feast, however, may simply be an anticipation of the new creation in which nothing, not even yeast, will be evil.

But he was a holy God, and she was a sinful people. Exodus 19 relates the story of her terrified approach: the mountain was covered in smoke, heaving and quaking violently; lightning flashed and thunder crashed so loudly that all trembled in dread fear. Israel was to keep her distance upon threat of death; only Moses could ascend the mountain to speak with YHWH.

It is no surprise, then, that the rabbis began to treat the period between Firstfruits and the Feast of Pentecost as a time of repentance before such a holy and awesome God and called it the time of "waiting for the gift." The gift was understood by the rabbis to be the Torah, the law of God. In the main synagogue prayer in later years, Pentecost was called "the time of the giving of our law."[2] In the fifty days leading up to the feast, it became customary for Israelites to read through the Torah and meditate upon Psalm 119, a song extolling the blessings of the law. Many memorized the psalm in its entirety as they "waited for the gift."

A Different Harvest

Like the three spring festivals, the Feast of Pentecost was a rehearsal celebration, one that anticipated a fuller redemption. God's people were to await a gift far more precious than the Torah.

This gift is mentioned in the only New Testament reference to the Feast of Pentecost, described in the opening verses of the book of Acts. Before describing the momentous events that would occur on Pentecost morning, Luke relates Jesus' parting words to his disciples (Acts 1:4): they were not to leave Jerusalem where God's people would congregate for the pilgrimage festival but rather were to "*wait for the gift* my Father promised, which you have heard me speak about" (emphasis added).

They were not to "count the *'omer*" as their ancestors had done, but wait with eager anticipation for the gift that would change everything. The gift of which Jesus spoke was not the Torah, but rather his Holy Spirit.

When Pentecost day arrived, it started with a bang. Reminiscent of the lightning, earthquake, and thunderous theophany at Sinai, Pentecost was accompanied by a "violent wind," tongues of fire, and Spirit-enabled speaking in languages in which the disciples had not been trained (Acts 2: 2–4). Peter, the spokesman for the apostles, explains the strange events by quoting the prophet Joel:

> 'In the last days, God says,
> I will pour out my Spirit on all people.

2 Hoffmann, *Das Buch Leviticus,* 224–40, as quoted in Noordtzij.

Your sons and daughters will prophesy,
  your young men will see visions,
  your old men will dream dreams.
Even on my servants, both men and women,
  I will pour out my Spirit in those days,
  and they will prophesy.
I will show wonders in the heaven above
  and signs on the earth below,
  blood and fire and billows of smoke.
The sun will be turned to darkness
and the moon to blood
  before the coming of the great and glorious day of the Lord.
And everyone who calls
  on the name of the Lord will be saved' (Acts 2:17–21).

The differences between a celebration focused on the Torah and one focused on the Holy Spirit were profound. The meaning of Pentecost would finally be anchored in the ministry of Messiah—not his ministry on earth, but rather his ministry from heaven where he sits at God's right hand, a ministry cloaked with earthshaking power. There may not have been a literal bloody moon that night, but the wonders and signs in heaven and on earth were none other than the outpouring of the Holy Spirit on all people. The significance of this event would rock the heavens and the earth.

In the first place, while Pentecost/Weeks had always been a harvest festival, it was only after the events of Acts 2 that the nature of the harvest could be understood. It was not a harvest of wheat and barley that was on God's mind and heart but rather a celebration of the harvest of redemption that had begun with Christ himself. He broke open the grave on Firstfruits as the "firstborn of the dead"—not just of dead bodies, but of what dead bodies evidenced: a dead-in-sin world (Revelation 1:5). And if he was the first sheaf, this fuller harvest was a bin buster, absolutely *cosmic* in scope. Peter's citation of Joel had hinted at redemption so grand that it included both young and old, men and women, and so expansive as to embrace all nations. "*Everyone* who calls on the name of the Lord will be saved" (Acts 2:21, emphasis added).

The method of gathering the harvest would be surprising too. Jesus had once conducted his earthly ministry in Galilee and Judea, walking the dusty roads from village to village, personally inviting people to himself by way of his teaching and his healing touch. Then he had explained that the kingdom of God was "within you," because its extent was tied to his physical presence (Luke 17:21). Then, the Spirit would be present in power only where he was physically present. But with Pentecost's arrival, Jesus would call people to himself from all over the world by means of a gospel borne by others. The bearers of the message would be the countless witnesses of a Spirit-filled church.

The apostles had been told to *wait for the gift,* but the gift was more than they had dreamed. "You will receive *power* when the Holy Spirit comes on you; and you will be my witnesses in Jerusalem, and in all Judea and Samaria, and to the ends of the earth" (Acts 1:8– 9, emphasis added). It's hard to miss his point: the Holy Spirit was poured out as the requisite empowerment that would drive the next phase—the missional phase—of God's redemptive work. Only in the power of the outpoured Spirit would the kingdom of God expand from Jesus' physical presence in first-century Palestine to the ends of the earth; only through the Spirit-emboldened preaching of ordinary men would the full reach of his redemption be made known.

Jesus had hinted at all this as he taught his disciples near the end of his ministry, explaining that "anyone who has faith in me will do what I have been doing. He will do even *greater things than these,* because I am going to the Father" (John 14:12, emphasis added). They had not understood. How could they, unschooled fishermen from Galilee, do greater things than their Master? He had raised the dead, healed the sick, and confounded the brilliant arguments of the most learned men in Israel.

On Pentecost, they would finally understand what he meant; the gift for which they were told to wait was a power that would change them and the world.

Languages Redeemed

The first surprise the unschooled apostles experienced was an ability to speak the gospel in the languages of the many nations gathered in Jerusalem for the feast. Through the gift of Pentecost tongues, Messiah Jesus began to redeem a world divided by language ever since the Tower of Babel. In that story, recorded in Genesis 11, mankind had acted in a united conspiracy. Forming a rebel alliance against the Creator King, men had aimed to usurp his place and take his glory for themselves by constructing a stair-stepped ziggurat that would reach all the way to the heavens. God foiled their conspiracy and broke their unity by confusing their language. He scattered them over the face of the earth, where the nations, and ultimately six thousand languages, remained fragmented for countless years.

But the gift of the Spirit would change all that. Pentecost's blessing overturned Babel's curse: languages would now serve the advancement of the kingdom of God. The conspiracy against the King of creation has been trumped by Jesus' strategy to bring a redemption that would reconcile, not divide, and make of all the nations of the earth one people for God's own pleasure (Revelation 5:9–10).

The miracle of the tongues at Pentecost must be understood in light of this dramatic connection between the Old Testament story and the New. The gift of tongues was much more than a private prayer language or a personal spiritual experience that confirms a second blessing beyond the gift of faith. Rather, the tongues of Pentecost had cosmic and strategic significance. More than mere sign, they were and are the *method* by which the Gentile world would open up to Christ's rule of grace.

The world of the nations had been, in the former days and by God's sovereign permission, held in the strong grip of Satan. Jesus had actually referred to him as the "prince of this world" (John 14:30; 16:11). But with Christ's ascension, Satan's permission to deceive the nations had come to an end.[3] All authority now belonged to Jesus (Matthew 28:18), and he commissioned his church to go into the world with the gospel of his kingdom. No longer would God be known only in Israel, the nations able to behold his glory only if they traveled to Jerusalem to see the gleaming white temple of Solomon, as the Queen of Sheba had once done. Evangelism then had been *centripetal,* drawing the nations in to the temple, the center of the world. Now the gospel of Christ would go to the nations with *centrifugal* force, propelled outward in the languages of all peoples.[4] Pentecost tongues involved real languages because real people needed to hear and understand the gospel, people like the "Parthians, Medes and Elamites; residents of Mesopotamia, Judea and Cappadocia, Pontus and Asia, Phrygia and Pamphylia, Egypt and the parts of Libya near Cyrene" (Acts 2:9–10).

The miracle of the tongues of Pentecost was not that unschooled fishermen spoke a spiritual tongue not even they understood or that the crowd suddenly could understand such a language, as Michael

3 The millennial kingdom in Revelation 20, as we shall see presently, is the kingdom Christ proclaimed to have already dawned in his first coming (Matthew 4:17; 12:28). His ascension marked his triumphal enthronement, and with it, the binding of Satan "so that he can no longer deceive the nations." This is the necessary corollary to Pentecost languages that would enable the kingdom's advancement to the ends of the earth (see Luke 11:20–21).

4 I learned this from my teacher, Professor Robert Recker.

Green suggests.[5] The miracle was that Peter and the others spoke real languages, earthly languages, tongues they had never before studied, and in so doing claimed all the cosmos for their Lord, Jesus the Messiah!

The Power of New Life

There is more. The first Pentecost, as the rabbinic scholars had concluded, was not celebrated in the harvest fields of Canaan, but at the base of Sinai. There, amid smoke, earthquake, and fear, Israel began her visitation with YHWH. The people saw the reality of their sinful condition in the bright light of his awesome holiness. They had been delivered by his strong arm; now they would learn that he was King and that his Word was the law of life.

As the stay at Sinai stretched out, Israel wrestled with the old idolatrous impulses again. Exodus 32:1 reports that Moses had been on the mountain a long time. While he was gone, Israel sinned. Impatient with "this fellow Moses" and needing to see her god and touch it with her hands, she commissioned the crafting of a golden calf, recreating the Egyptian bull-god Apis, whom YHWH had already crushed. The people conscripted Aaron, God's high priest and Moses' own brother, to forge the idol of gold, using bounty the Egyptians had pressed into their hands on their way out of the land.

When Moses descended the mountain with the two tablets of the law in hand and saw the orgy of sin in full bloom, he shattered the copies of the covenant, not in a fit of pique or temper, but in painful recognition that the covenant of God had already been broken. He first confronted his brother, who, in an Adam-like act of blame-shifting that is as bald as it is creative, shrugged: "They gave me the gold, and I threw it into the fire, and *out came this calf!*" (Exodus 32:24, emphasis added). With righteous anger, God sent the Levites through the camp with swords in hand, each "killing his brother and friend and neighbor (v. 27)." That day, three thousand died.

Well over a millennium later, at another Pentecost, the enthroned Messiah sent his Holy Spirit to the disciples, empowering them to preach the gospel using a weapon of a different sort. The "sword of the Spirit"

5 In a world where Greek was the universal language, Green thinks Peter preached in Greek and was understood by all. The miracle of Pentecost, he argues, had to do with the *glossolalia*, the unique spiritual language of praise miraculously given to all the disciples, miraculously understood by the crowd through the gift of interpretation. *Thirty Years That Changed the World: The Book of Acts for Today* (Grand Rapids: Eerdman's, 1993), 252–253.

would cut even more sharply than levitical steel, slicing to the core of every issue and every soul, cutting so deep as to expose and judge even the thoughts and attitudes of the heart. But when the Spirit's sword flashes, *life* results, not death. In an astonishing display of divine grace, Sinai was reversed. Precisely three thousand were saved.

Paul explains it simply. "The letter kills, the Spirit gives life" (2 Corinthians 3:6).

The law never could save, and the law never will. It can serve only to highlight its own impotence, one rooted in the corrupt hearts of those who try to obey in the strength of their own flesh. After preaching a very practical message on overcoming temptation one Sunday, Bryan Chapell was confronted by an old man who frankly observed, "It won't work . . . People do precisely what they love, and until they have a greater love for the things of God than the things of this world, they will not be able to stop."[6]

The old man was right. The law—with all its techniques, boundaries, and accountability relationships—cannot rescue us. Chapell reflects on why that is. "Could it really be that simple? Is our power in our passions? . . . Do we simply do what we most love to do, and thus the power for spiritual change is found in the affections of the heart? If that is so, then the love that motivates us is actually the power that drives us. Why we do what we do is also how we do what we do. If why I serve God is also how I serve God, then greater love precedes greater power. And, in fact, since we will only and always do what we love the most, then greater love is the means to greater power."[7]

At the beginning of this chapter, I told JD's story. JD had laws, but the laws killed him: they exposed his sin and, as Romans 7:8 reveals, actually inflamed his sinfulness, provoking and producing more of the same. JD also had religion, but his religion could not absolve his guilt: JD knew from painful experience that he would sin again, that he could not stop patterns that had owned his life for decades. What JD needed was a new heart, one driven by a new fuel source, the Spirit's power to change him from within. His only hope was metamorphosis, a transformation so radical that he would love God more than he loved the sins his heart had craved for so long.

To people like JD, the gospel of Pentecost proclaims, in letters writ large, that there is a peace to be found at the end of the law's internal

6 *Ephesians* (Phillipsburg, NJ: P&R Publishing, 2009), 150.
7 Ibid.

anguish, a peace that comes with the power to change.

Keeping the Feast Today

The Feast of Pentecost bears a vital message for the church of God in the twenty-first century. Remembering the Feast of Pentecost and what it teaches us about the gospel is an intensely ***personal*** exercise. It begins with "preaching the gospel to yourself each day," Martin Luther's counsel to a people like us whose heart-default would always be one of guilt and fear before a holy God. Each of us needs daily reminders of our identity as justified, forgiven, and adopted sons of God, or we will run home to fear and self-doubt, stuck permanently in the diagnosis of "sinner."

People caught up in that loop experience daily the misery of what Paul calls the "law of the law": all that the law can do is expose their sin and produce more of the same.[8] They see in themselves only the impotence of the flesh, never the triumph of the Spirit. Their lives mirror fictional Gollum, the wretched creature in Tolkien's Lord of the Rings, who has forgotten human joys like friendship and love and knows only treachery and violence in his slave-like quest to possess the ring of power. Like him—one who can barely remember what he once was—they lose touch with what God made them to be and what they have become again in Christ. Like him, they argue within their souls in a pathetic and schizophrenic dialogue: the flesh always scheming for the precious ring, the spirit longing for dignity, purpose, and rest. Like him, they are always warring but never finding peace.

Keeping the feast of Pentecost today is also a *communal* activity of the church, one that is both mysterious and strategic. Pentecost had demonstrated that Christ's ongoing redemptive work would be tied to the gift of human tongues. That gift continues to serve the same redemptive purpose today, enabling missionaries, teachers, and Bible translators across the globe to announce the gospel of God.

> As young adults, Doug and PJ committed their lives to the work of Bible translation. They went to Mali, West Africa, some fifteen years ago, committed to providing a translation of the Bible to the Fulani nomads whose oral language—the Fulfulde dialect—was not well documented. They knew that the task would be huge and would require a lifetime commitment; but they also knew that the

8 As Lloyd-Jones's thoughtful exposition of Romans 7 points out in *Romans: An Exposition of Chapters 7:1–8:4* (Grand Rapids: Zondervan Publishing Corp., 1973).

power of the Spirit was greater than the frustrating limitations of language. They possessed the gift of tongues, the divine enablement to work with languages in ways most of us simply cannot.

Their first task was to learn French, a language that would serve as a bridge to the people and cultures of West Africa. Next, in French, they had to build relationships of trust and respect with the Fulani tribesmen of Mali, relationships that would allow them to learn the vocabulary and nuances of the tribal tongue. The third step in the process would be to document the tribal language, actually build a dictionary, then teach the written tongue back to the people in their community, most of whom knew their language only orally. Only then could they confidently do the work of translating the individual books of the Bible into that tongue.

The next stage of their work also required Pentecost gifts: from the original Greek or Hebrew the Word of God flowed into an English-thinking brain, was then translated into the Fulfulde tongue so as to enable communication with tribesmen who did not know English, then translated back word for word into the national tongue (French) to allow biblical consultants to verify the accuracy of the translation. At last, final adjustments would be made into the translation into the tribal tongue.

When at long last they delivered a finished New Testament to the leaders of the tribe, it was a day of unbridled celebration.
Leaders and tribal members, translators, missionaries, and singers came from far and wide to feast, worship, and rejoice before the Lord for what he had enabled by the gift of tongues through his Pentecost Spirit. Many friends and family on other parts of the globe joined in the communal festivities in spirit.

The gift of tongues is a restless one, relentlessly pushing outward in new directions. Doug and PJ have not sat on their laurels but are already driven by the Spirit's gift into new dimensions of service. It should not be surprising that their new ministry reveals a new and technological dimension to the Pentecostal gift, for they serve now as consultants and advisors, not only in West Africa, but across that continent and beyond, helping missionaries and translators everywhere leverage powerful computer programs to aid in the development of more rapid yet accurate Bible translations for the thousands of languages that still do not yet have the Scriptures.

Sending missionaries and translators to the ends of the earth is only part of the joy of the Feast the church celebrates. Pentecost also challenges local churches to view the purpose of their very existence as *missional,* for Pentecost as a modern feast of faith not only celebrates the power of the Spirit, but also his *strategy.* In the twenty-first century, the ambient culture in the West has become as pagan and post-Christian as the first century was pre-Christian. Our culture, long draped with the vestiges of Christendom, if not with vital faith, has become one that no longer knows or believes the Word of God, no longer understands the power of grace, and does not understand the good news at all. Local churches must, as a matter of intentional purpose, be dynamic communities of believers who live in the power of the Spirit of Pentecost, individually and communally bearing the Word, modeling the grace and joy of the Lord that transformed them, *translating* the gospel through relationships and deeds into the language of the neighborhood. Their holiness, passion for justice and righteousness, love and compassion, genuine fellowship, and even their confession and repentance of sin (all less than perfect) bear unexpected yet authentic testimony to the gospel of Jesus the Christ and demonstrate that his kingdom is on the move.[9]

The gospel is not only personal, but also cosmic; not only private, but also global. As previously noted, Jesus once explained both the motive and scope of gospel redemption, saying simply, "God so loved the *cosmos*" (John 3:16). In that familiar passage, John used a Greek word for "world" that connotes the creation itself in all its broad dimensions. But God also loves the nations. The Feast of Pentecost embodies the other Greek word for world, *ecumene*, a reference to the world of peoples. Mankind's unity was frustrated by sin at Babel and has been fragmented by language, color, economics, and politics ever since. That unity is being restored in the Christ who overturned Babel's curse. All kinds of people—representing diverse cultures and tongues—find one life, one hope, and one voice in Jesus the Messiah. For he "purchased men for God from every tribe and language and people and nation" and "made them to be a kingdom and priests to serve our God" (Revelation 5:9–10).

Israel had been the rootstock into which all the branches of the nations would be grafted. She was called first; but—as God assured Abraham in

9 Usually we think of *missional* as attractional—how can we attract people to our churches? But in a post- Christian world, almost nothing will attract pagans to churches except believers' lives that model the gospel with integrity. We must go to the pagans as the first-century church did and build intentional relationships with them for gospel purposes.

Genesis 12:3—she was rootstock only, not the whole tree. Her calling would be expanded from a land to the globe, from the bloodline of Abraham to the faith line of a church made up of Jew and Gentile, male and female, bond and free. Most importantly, to reach all the nations of the earth with the good news of the kingdom of God, the church would not convey a system of religion, a temple complete with priests and sacrifices. She would need another instrument entirely.

She would be given a trumpet.

Questions for Further Study and Discussion

1. The death of three thousand in the incident of the golden calf and the salvation of three thousand at Pentecost in Acts 2 punctuate the biblical claim: "The letter kills, but the Spirit gives life" (2 Corinthians 3:6). Using Romans 7:7–20, explain why the law is impotent. With Ephesians 5:18, pray today (as a person, as a group) for the powerful filling of the Spirit to enable fruitful Christian living.
2. Various Christian communities view tongues in different ways. What does your church teach regarding tongues? How does this chapter's explanation of the tongues of Pentecost help (or hinder) your understanding of this gift?
3. Is your church missional? If it is, what special skills has God granted you that have enabled you to communicate the gospel to your neighbors in the post-Christian world in which you live? If not, what new "language" do you think you must learn in order to connect with them?

Chapter 6

The Trumpet Shall Sound . . .

The Feast of Trumpets

Leviticus 23:23–25

I like trumpets. I played one for many years in my youth and actually thought about studying music and playing professionally. God adjusted my sense of calling through a baseball game in which a bat met up with a few of my teeth; I've always viewed it as one of his more creative ways to get a stubborn young man into the ministry. I seldom play any more, and never very well, but I still love the instrument and the pieces written for it. I'm enchanted by the Haydn, Telemann, and Vivaldi concerti. I love old jazz and blues greats like Louis Armstrong. I am addicted to anything by Wynton Marsalis, who plays jazz like few others and yet crosses over to win Grammy after Grammy for his classical brilliance.

One thing is true about a trumpet: it's loud. If you play one, you never forget that truth. If you make one mistake in a concert, you can't cover it up by smoothly pretending it didn't happen. Everyone already knows. Our city's symphony orchestra program includes two dozen violins but lists only three trumpets. It doesn't need more.

Perhaps because of their piercing sound, trumpets have not always been used for musical and entertainment purposes. For most of history, trumpets of varying kinds served more utilitarian purposes. They blew fanfares that marked royal events; they were an important means of battlefield communication, signaling the command to attack, to retreat, which strategy to employ, and which weapons to use; and, of course, trumpets were used as the original emergency warning system: when the trumpet blew, the city was alerted to impending danger.

The sound of the trumpet is the focus of the Feast of Trumpets, the first of the trio of fall feasts celebrated in the seventh month of Israel's calendar, around October today. As the spring feasts found their fulfillment in Christ's earthly ministry and Pentecost in his Spirit's outpouring, the fall festivals find their fulfillment in the work of the church. The impact of her gospel would be twofold: first, it would bring transformation to the lives of people today; second, it will change all things when Jesus returns to complete his redemptive program.

The Feast of Trumpets commenced on the first day of the seventh month. Remember, beginning with the exodus, deliverance—and not agriculture—would serve as the axis around which Israel's life turned. God had relocated the beginning of the new year from the fall to the spring to coincide with Passover deliverance (Exodus 12:1–2). Over the centuries, however, Israel gradually lost sight of the redemptive purpose of her election as the chosen people of God. As she did, the feasts in the seventh month that were to celebrate and mark God's redemptive harvest reverted to their original agricultural focus. Over the centuries, the Feast of Trumpets, so named by God himself in Leviticus 23, came to be known by another name. *Rosh HaShanah, or* "head of the year," was merely a new year's celebration.

To understand the character of this feast as it was originally commissioned by God, we must return to its first purpose, one attuned to the peculiar horn whose sound was central to the celebration.

Trumpet Voices

Few understand that different trumpets, like people, have different voices. The trumpet I played as a youth was technically a cornet, an instrument slightly shorter and a bit mellower in tone. Years later, a friend showed up for worship practice toting a flugelhorn. Still considered a trumpet, it had a larger bell and softer bends and produced a fuller and richer tone. One year, a symphony trumpeter showed up for our Christmas Eve service toting a piccolo trumpet. So tiny it looked like a toy, its bright notes added a soaring countermelody high above our congregational singing. It was magnificent. Each of these instruments makes the sound of a trumpet, but each has its own voice. So did trumpets in Bible times.

Actually, the biblical word for trumpets likewise needs a bit of definition. In Israel's life, there were two distinct kinds. There were silver trumpets, *hotsotsera*, which were metallic instruments, a pair of which had been hammered out by a craftsman at God's command (Numbers 10:1–10). They were used mostly for communal purposes: they summoned Israel to assemble and communicated organizational signals for her travel from camp to camp through the desert.

More important to Israel's faith life was another trumpet, the ram's horn, or shofar. The Feast of Trumpets (literally *Yom t'Ruah,* or "day for blowing") was a festival originally structured around the sound of these instruments. Like trumpets today, shofarim came in several voices. Some were large, deep-throated horns with a rich baritone sound, while intermediate horns provided a tenor voice and smaller ones a higher pitch, layering piercing top notes in the alto or even soprano range. Through the centuries, tradition allowed the Levites to fashion liturgical instruments from the horns of rams or antelope but never from oxen or calves, which some think is related to the incident of the golden calf. The diversity of horn material added to the blend of sounds and pitches. All were fitted with mouthpieces of silver or gold, and all were played by Levites who were skilled at what they were doing. The sound of large choirs of horns all day long, from dawn to dusk, must have been amazing to hear.

Such was the Feast of Trumpets. It was insistent, it was beautiful, it was majestic, and it was loud.

Not only did trumpets play in different voices and octaves, but the Mishnah identifies at least three distinct *melodies.* One of these they called sustained, another quavering, and the third prolonged.[1] There were even more distinctions. On the day of the feast, several of the trumpet solos took on a special character and marked significant moments. The first trumpet announced the beginning of the feast and called Israel to assemble. Later in Israel's history, that first trumpet would serve as the formal proclamation of the new moon or the new agricultural year. The last trumpet would, of course, signal the conclusion of the feast of the blowing of the trumpet. And on the tenth day of the seventh month, known as the Day of Atonement, or *Yom Kippur,* the great trumpet would sound.

Our God Reigns!

The sound of the ram's horn bore a significance rooted in redemptive history. When Abraham was called to sacrifice Isaac on an altar (Genesis 22), it was a ram, provided as the substitute for his son, that

1 The Mishnah, Rosh Ha-Shanah 4:9, 194.

provided deliverance through blood. From that moment on, the horn of the ram awakened and renewed that memory. Its sound announced God's presence.

On one hand, that sound claimed sovereignty.

The president of the United States is introduced with a simple trumpet fanfare, played three times, followed by the familiar strains of "Hail to the Chief." Similarly, the blowing of the *shofar* accompanied events of State in Old Testament Israel. Israel's human kings, like David and Solomon, were crowned to its sounds. But David's royal line served under Israel's true Sovereign. She was herself the visible evidence of God's kingdom on earth. Camped at the base of Sinai, summoned to the mountain by the sound of the shofar (Exodus 19:16), Israel came to meet the God who had redeemed her and who therefore claimed royal rights to rule as her Lord.

God claimed more than Israel, of course. The earth is the Lord's, as Israel would learn to sing in Psalm 24. Yahweh refused to be thought a mere territorial deity like the idols of the nations.

> God has ascended amid shouts of joy,
>   the LORD amid the sounding of [shofarim].
> Sing praises to God, sing praises;
>   sing praises to our King, sing praises.
> *For God is the King of all the earth . . .*
> *God reigns over the nations* (Psalm 47:5–8, emphasis added).

In addition to sovereignty, the blowing of the shofar signaled a call to remember. Not only would the horn bring to mind the story of Abraham and the Isaac incident, but also many other stories of God's track record of grace would immediately spring to mind. Think of the tale of Jericho's fall. When Israel marched around the city seven times (Joshua 6), that march was accompanied by the sound of the ram's horn. The trumpet's sound invoked YHWH's intervention and summoned Israel to act with faith's courage. When the walls fell, the message was clear: they tumbled by God's mighty hand. Israel had learned that her security lay not in walls but in *him*. The preserved ruins would stand as mute testimony to that truth; the sound of the trumpet would actuate the memory of his mighty works in a powerful way.

As time would soon tell, Israel would *not* remember God; her hardening heart would repeatedly forget the God who could never forget her (Isaiah 49:14–15). Her failure to remember meant she had broken covenant with her God. Moses had once solemnly intoned, "Be careful that you do not forget the LORD, who brought you out of Egypt . . ."

(Deuteronomy 6:12). But she did forget, and when she did, God sent his prophets. Their voice was likened to the sound of the ram's horn warning the city of doom. The prophets—"watchmen on the walls" of the city—were sent to rouse the people to repent before the arrival of the King. Danger was coming, the kind of danger that justice always brings to the unjust. The Righteous Judge of heaven and earth was on the move:

Sound the trumpet in Tekoa!
Raise the signal . . .
For disaster looms out of the north,
even terrible destruction.
I will destroy the Daughter of Zion . . ." (Jeremiah 6:1–2, emphasis added).

The Celebration in the First Century

By the first century, the shift from *Yom t'Ruah* (the "day for blowing" the trumpets) to *Rosh HaShanah* (the "head of the year") was complete, bringing with it not only a new name but also a complete shift of focus. No longer was the Feast of Trumpets viewed as a celebration of God's redemptive work and a call to worship the King in repentance and faith. Instead, it had become one of many repetitious new moon celebrations, this one special only in that it also signaled the arrival of the new year. The difference is significant: key to *Yom t'Ruah* but missing from *Rosh HaShanah* was the sound of the presence of God, the decidedly redemptive focus that gave the feast its unique character.

Part of the reason for this shift in focus may be that no single redemptive event in the Old Testament history of Israel connected the people's hearts to the blowing of the trumpet. Passover, Unleavened Bread, and Firstfruits were all anchored in the exodus from Egypt and found fulfillment in Christ's death, burial, and resurrection. Eventually, Pentecost found its type at Sinai and its completion in the outpouring of the Spirit. But not Trumpets. No references in the Gospels overtly link Jesus' earthly ministry to the ancient feast.

None, that is, unless you peel the text back a bit more. The sound of the trumpet was, in fact, critical to the ministry of Messiah; it just had a different resonance.

With the dawn of the New Testament, God's trumpet would still sound sovereignty, would still call God's people to remember and thus worship, and would still summon sinners to repent. It would, in other words, still serve to announce the presence and rule of God. But the Sovereign himself, and his reign of grace, could now be more fully revealed. His name is Jesus, and his coming to earth was the arrival of

God's kingdom. During his earthly ministry, he spoke of this pointedly: "If I drive out demons by the Spirit of God, then the kingdom of God *has come* upon you" (Matthew 12:28, emphasis added). Later in Matthew's gospel, just prior to the Great Commission (Matthew 28:19–20), Jesus expanded his claim, now affirming universal sovereignty: "All authority in heaven and on earth has been given to me" (v. 18). By virtue of the cross and the resurrection, he would ascend to heaven to assume authority over a world that, until then, had been in the grip of rebel hands. All of God's creation is now to be under Christ's gracious rule. The land of Canaan had once been claimed for the LORD to the sound of Joshua's *shofarim*. Jesus' similar claim is punctuated by the sound of another trumpet.

Trumpet the Gospel

What trumpet accompanied the ministry of Messiah in the first century? Surprisingly, it was the preaching of the gospel.

In the Greek language, the principal verb for preaching is *kerusso*; what is preached is the *kerugma*. The word denotes the herald's cry, cloaked in royal authority, which declares the king's arrival and calls the people to receive him. The ancient shofar always connected to human voice. When a "watchman . . . blows the trumpet" from the walls of Zion (in the compelling metaphor in Ezekiel 33:3), he preaches. "Hear the word I speak and give them warning from me" (v. 7).

In the first centuries of the Christian church, *kerusso* preaching was done by men set apart by ordination, men called apostles, prophets, evangelists, pastors, and teachers. Sometimes they preached in synagogues, but more frequently on street corners, in marketplaces, or in meeting places like Mars Hill in Athens where Paul preached Christ to the Epicurean and Stoic philosophers of the day (Acts 17). In such settings, the preaching of the apostles was pointed: God the King had come in the person of Jesus the Messiah. The announcement was gracious, for it offered redemption; yet it was insistent, for it demanded the hearts of all who heard.

First-century audiences—both religious Jews and pagan Gentiles—seemed to get the point. The early verses of Acts 18 narrate the story of Paul's preaching to the Jews "that Jesus was the Christ" (v. 5). The crowds responded vigorously; they opposed him and "became abusive." In the next chapter, Luke elaborates. Paul's preaching, a trumpet solo of sorts, provoked a riot that threatened the safety of both Paul and his traveling companions. There is no doubt that those who heard Paul preach truly understood that God was staking his claim on their lives and their cities, and they wanted none of it.

Others who heard the preaching of the gospel believed. Their response also reveals that they understood the seriousness of the trumpet call of God. Acts 19:18–19 tells of some who "came and openly confessed their evil deeds. A number who had practiced sorcery brought their scrolls together and burned them publicly. When they calculated the value of the scrolls, the total came to fifty thousand drachmas." Now this was a serious response to preaching! A drachma was an entire day's wage; the bonfire consumed the total annual income of 140 workers. It was a vast fortune.

In the early church, not all "trumpet players" of the gospel were professionals. All believers understood that it was their duty to "preach," and they did it as naturally as breathing. Self-conscious ambassadors for Christ, these early believers lived life "on the witness stand." The New Testament uses a different Greek word for this form of preaching: *evangelizo* describes the witness and testimony borne by all believers. Driven out from Jerusalem by persecution, they took the gospel to the ends of the earth and "preached [evangelized] the word wherever they went" (Acts 8:4).

Empowered and emboldened by the Spirit of Pentecost, led by her apostles and preachers, yet involving every member, the early church moved into the pagan cultures of all nations to sound the claim of her King: "Our God reigns! Receive him! Repent of your sins, believe in his Son, and worship the King!"

A Muted Bell

Preaching as we know it in the twenty-first century has fallen on hard times. To most people outside the church, preaching is a synonym for pushy, self-righteous talk that offers little of value. To many in the church, preaching is viewed as a neural anesthetic.

The problem is not merely one of style: it matters little whether the preacher wears a suit or is more casual, whether he stands at a pulpit or uses a music stand, whether his message is very short or quite lengthy. The problem is that the church—not to mention the world in which the church is to labor for the King—has lost sight of the *nature* and *character* of preaching.

In the New Testament, preaching is always the headline, never merely the small print. Preaching is always a bold announcement that the King has come, that his coming will truly and radically change things, and that he has the right to claim royal authority over every creature in his realm. Preaching is thus always two dimensional: a herald's cry, a trumpet blast, a sound moving directly from God's mouth to your ears and your heart.

Preaching, according to the Bible's definition of the term, is never a talk about a subject. It is never a three-point conversation: a message from me (point A) to you (point B) about a subject or topic (point C).[2] Preaching is never merely a Sunday morning homily for people who have reserved family seats for the eleven o'clock service (but, more importantly, reservations for lunch or the football game afterwards). The difference between this and real preaching is the difference between a clear trumpet sound and one muffled by a mute in the horn's bell.

Biblically defined, preaching is always grace driven, for it declares the person and work of Jesus the Messiah as Savior. It is also royal, for it proclaims that Jesus the Lord wants your life and calls you to follow him. Preaching is clothed with ambassadorial authority, for the preacher represents the King. Sometimes it is a royal irritation, for it moves unapologetically from the indicative to the imperative, sticking the nose of God's Word into your life. Preaching doesn't merely try to talk you into accepting helpful information as if you were buying term life insurance. Instead, it insists that you must answer the King in faith, repenting where sinful, changing where disobedient, following where called. Good preaching just stands there—like the King's messenger it is—fully expecting an answer. Preaching, biblically understood, always provokes a crisis in the life of the one who hears it.

This is true because preaching is conditioned by the character of the good news it bears. Jesus came preaching "repent, for the kingdom of heaven is near" (Matthew 4:17). He did not mean that the kingdom might be at hand if people believed his sermon. He did not invite people to consider whether or not the kingdom might come one day soon if only they would behave themselves. He proclaimed it as fact, for his coming had inaugurated it. On the basis of that fact and as evidence of the change of regime his arrival brought, he cast out demons, healed the sick, made strong the limbs of the lame, restored sight to the blind and hearing to the deaf. He explained himself wherever he went: "If I drive out demons by the finger of God, then the kingdom of God has come to you" (Luke 11:20).

2 I am indebted for this insight to Jay Adams, *Preaching with Purpose* (Grand Rapids, Michigan: Baker Books, 1982), 42ff.

To put it simply, in sending Christ, God was reclaiming the creation that had once been his "very good" dominion. It had been led into rebellion, but he was taking it back, making right what sin had made wrong in all the world. That is what God had been planning since the dawn of time.

Beautiful Feet

In sending the church into all the world with the gospel on her lips and in her life, the King who once claimed "all authority in heaven and on earth" was not just sending out *reporters*. The word of preaching is itself the legal vehicle of repossession. Biblically understood, preaching is endowed with power of attorney; it doesn't just speak *about* Christ, but *brings* Christ to the hearer. Preaching is thus actually redemptive.

I've always been struck by the ancient practice of executing a runner who carried bad news to the king. It worked like this: if a battle on a distant plain were lost on June 1, the king in his throne room would not hear about it until a runner arrived with news from the battlefield on June 3. Ironically, it was not the blood-curdling cries of the battlefield, but the messenger's voice that actually brought pain to the hearts of the king and his people. Because the messenger brought the bad news, it was understood that he caused the pain. Thus, he was summarily executed. We get the metaphor "killing the messenger" from the custom.

Conversely, if the battle had been won on June 1, the messenger who brought good news to the city on June 3 was feted. As a trained long-distance runner, he would probably have been a skinny young man with prominent ribs and calloused feet, unsuited for hand to hand combat and almost certainly no famous battlefield hero. Yet he was given a laurel wreath and was rewarded with fame and fortune as if he had slain thousands. Why? He had brought good news! This, the flipside of "killing the messenger," is what lies behind Isaiah's exultant cry:

> How beautiful on the mountains
> are the feet of those who bring good news,
> who proclaim peace,
> who bring good tidings, who proclaim salvation, who say to Zion,
> "Your God reigns!" (52:7).

Isaiah knew full well about the dirty, bloody, smelly feet of mountain runners. Yet, he could rejoice, for he knew the role these feet would have in bringing good news to the hearers of the gospel, news that would change their lives forever.

The preaching of the gospel does that. God had not only sent Jesus to earth to die as the Lamb of God around AD 33, but now he sends the church to tell the world about it twenty-one centuries later. The voice of the church *actuates* good news for all who hear and believe. God's salvation had been accomplished in Jesus' cross and resurrection. But it is the *news* about the cross and resurrection, the good news brought by gospel preaching, that actually saves anyone who believes. Paul's words in Romans 10:17 are more than tactical counsel; they reveal a profound reality: "Faith comes from hearing." First Peter 1:23–25 goes even further: the gospel preached is the seed of rebirth!

In today's world, we usually don't "kill the messenger"; yet stories persist that validate the point that it is the news that makes the victory (or the defeat) real to the hearer. Perhaps you've heard the true stories about Japanese soldiers, years after World War II ended, still alert, maintaining military readiness in bases located deep in the honeycombed caves of remote Philippine Islands. Their communications cut off, they had never received word that the war was over. Only when they heard the news from reliable sources could they rest; only then would they lay down their arms.

Several chapters ago, I related my experience with acute leukemia. Allow me to tell you a bit more of that story.

> I left the hospital on February 25, 1998, returning frequently for blood tests—at first weekly, then bi-weekly, then monthly. I was beginning to feel quite healthy.
>
> Then I met Carol.
>
> We began dating about eighteen months after I had been released from the hospital, and it was not long before I was smitten. Planning to propose marriage, I felt obligated to do some "due diligence" on my health before popping the question. (It was like checking the horse's teeth before buying the nag, only I was the nag.)
>
> When I asked my doctor to perform a bone marrow biopsy, he looked at me as if I'd lost my mind. I'd already endured four such tests; each involved a painful procedure during which the doctor drilled a one-eighth-inch hole in the pelvis bone just to the side of the spine. A device is inserted into the opening, and marrow is suctioned out. No painkiller is effective for such a site, so none is used except a topical anesthetic on the surface of the skin. Bottom line: it hurts. The upside is that the test provides a more thorough analysis of the state of the bone marrow, which produces blood cells, and therefore is a much more accurate diagnostic tool than a mere blood test. Before proposing a new life with Carol, I wanted as good a look at the state of my health as I could get.

The doctor shook his head but finally agreed to do the test. It didn't take long; it did hurt. I hobbled out of his office, drove home, took some Tylenol, and waited.

It was a long day before I would get the report. I knew that what I would hear when he called, be it good news or bad, would be evidence of cell activity already long at work in my body. But when the doctor himself called, I inhaled a breath and held it. "You're clean, John. Congratulations! Go get married!"

I exhaled slowly and then shed a tear of joy.

We had a party that night, a party occasioned by more than healthy marrow cells. It was a party occasioned by the arrival of the good news.

Gospel and Law

The trumpet call of God in preaching is like that phone call. It brings—actually makes alive—the joy of the gospel in those who hear and believe. Through the Word preached, Christ actually gives grace to those who hear and believe. But the Word of God also comes with royal character; it comes as God's law by which men and women of faith must now live. It is, after all, the word of a King, not just information.

Much of today's preaching has lost that royal dynamic. This is partly due to an inaccurate understanding of the relationship between law and gospel, one that drives a wedge between the two, thus reducing gospel to a mere offer.[3] It is also partly due to the relentless impact of television on this culture, one that actually changes the way human minds process information. Marva Dawn observes that "television has habituated its watchers to a low information-action ratio" so that "people are accustomed to 'learning' good ideas (even from sermons) and then doing nothing about them."[4]

Yet preaching—correctly understood—is so critical a step in the gospel's redemptive program that Jesus lists it as the third leg of the redemptive tripod, inseparably linking his death and resurrection with the communication of the good news of both. "The Christ will suffer

3 C. Veenhof, writing of the interaction of law and gospel, suggests that "time and again the church has taken a wrong turn in this regard, to the serious detriment of the life of faith." See his *Prediking en Uitverkiezing* (Kampen: J. H. Kok, 1959), 215–234, translated as *The Word of God and Preaching,* trans. Nelson D. Kloosterman (Dyer, IN: Mid-America Reformed Seminary, 1987).

4 Marva J. Dawn, *Reaching Out without Dumbing Down* (Grand Rapids, Michigan: William B. Eerdmans Publishing Co., 1995), 21.

and rise from the dead on the third day, and repentance and forgiveness of sins will be preached in his name to all nations" (Luke 24:46–7).

Keeping the Feast

So how might we keep the feast? Should we actually celebrate in the twenty-first century an ancient festival that celebrates the sound of the trumpet call of God? Allow me to suggest a few things, all of which involve a committed engagement with the royal preaching of the gospel.

First, make sure you hear the sound of the trumpet regularly. By this, without apology, I call you to submit yourself willingly to faithful preaching in a gospel-driven church. I mean the kind of preaching that reminds you of what God has done in Christ, then applies that good news directly to the broken places of your heart, your life, and your city. Let me be blunt: if you're not transformed by the gospel preached in your church—if it isn't meddling with your beliefs, behavior, and motives; if it isn't continuously molding your life, both liberating you from sin's grip and showing you the joy of following Christ—then I dare say it's time to look for another church.

Second, make sure you are involved in a church that understands her calling to sound the trumpet to your town or city. Many in America mistakenly think of the church in business terms. Its neighbors (our world) are customers whom we attract and service in order to achieve and mark success. But Jesus' paradigm is different. The church exists for the world, bears her cross for the world, lives for the world, and dies for the world. The local church is a congregation chosen out of the world by Christ to live in the world for Christ. Her very life models the gospel she bears. Her existence serves as the herald's cry to the city or town in which God has placed her.[5]

Third, *you* must preach. Reminding your congregation to sound the trumpet to the city in her pulpit and by her communal witness will sound like self-righteous nagging if you are not bearing the gospel yourself in the impact zone in which God has placed you. Like first-century believers who carried the word wherever they went, you must

5 Lesslie Newbigin is insightful: "How is it possible that the gospel should be credible, that people should come to believe that the power which has the last word in human affairs is represented by a man hanging on a cross? I am suggesting that the only answer, the only hermeneutic of the gospel, is a congregation of men and women who believe it and live by it." Lesslie Newbigin, "The Gospel in a Pluralist Society," in *Lesslie Newbigin, Missionary Theologian: A Reader,* ed. Paul Weston (Grand Rapids: William B. Eerdman's Publishing Company, 2006), 152.

bear the gospel to your world, fulfilling a calling that has both verbal and ethical dimensions. Peter explains, beginning with the verbal: "You are a chosen people, a royal priesthood, a holy nation, a people belonging to God, that you may *declare* the praises of him who called you out of darkness into his wonderful light" (1 Peter 2:9, emphasis added). In the next verses, he explains the ethical: "*Live such good lives* among the pagans that, though they accuse you of doing wrong, they may see your good deeds and glorify God" (v. 12, emphasis added).

You and I are called, in short, to tell the story of the gospel, the story of Christ's redemption. One of the ways we do that is by telling our own story of redemption by his grace.

I've told many stories in these pages, but I have not told yours. Your story is unique, and only you can tell it. Each of our stories possesses gospel force when it is authentic. Perhaps yours is a marriage story, a tale of forgiveness after infidelity that models Christ's forgiveness of unfaithful people like us. That kind of story gives your neighbors—and their marriages—hope founded in Christ and not in counseling techniques or divorce courts. Maybe yours is a story involving cancer, one that speaks frankly of mortality but points to a hope in Christ beyond this fleshly existence. Perhaps yours is a story set in the context of work, one that tells of redemption from the idols of power and wealth and success that hold so many in bondage. Or maybe yours is one of sex, of looking for love in all the wrong places but finding real love only when you found Christ, a lover who accepts you by grace through faith alone.

Dan Allender's book *To Be Told* masterfully demonstrates just how you can come to "write your story" for others in your world to read, a story both of redemption and grace, one that trumpets the love and grace of God.

Using your own story for God's purposes is precisely Paul's point in 2 Corinthians 1:3–11. When God walks you through the misery, sin, and hurt of life, he does not let you off the hook, never again requiring you to think back on your guilt or pain. Instead, he calls you to minister out of the painful and humbling memory of that very weakness. Once saved, believers are not permitted to glue on a veneer of respectability and wholeness as if they had never been a wretched mess. They are called instead never to forget what they have been saved *from*, and always remember what they have been saved *for*, so that they can point others still caught in the weeds to the hope and healing God's grace provides in Christ. Allender models what he says, referring honestly to his pre-Christ days of drug use. His frankness is quite remarkable, but it is what makes his words so compelling, his message so convicting.

Fourth, keeping the Feast of Trumpets demands a big vision. Since Christ is Lord of all, the trumpet must sound across the entire globe. This requires that believers be deeply committed to the training and sending of gospel preachers everywhere the Lord is not known. The sixteenth-century Heidelberg Catechism actually identified this commitment as the first duty of keeping the Sabbath day holy: "First, that the gospel ministry and education for it be maintained . . ." That may involve contributing to Bible colleges and seminaries, supporting Bible translation work, or generously funding creative methods of training that reach the growing percentage of the world's population that has no access to traditional education. An example is Third Millenium Ministries, based in Orlando, Florida, and led by Richard Pratt. He left a successful professorship in a traditional seminary to head up a ministry that delivers "seminary in a box" training via audio, video, on-line, and print media to the ninety percent of the world's pastors and teachers around the globe who do not have access to training structures of brick and mortar.

Keeping the Feast of Trumpets especially requires that you pray. I wish that all churches would pray for their preachers the way the Brooklyn Tabernacle does for their pastor, Jim Cymbala.[6] The members of the church know experientially that every time their pastor mounts the pulpit with God's Word he will be confronting the spiritual forces of evil in New York with the royal claims of the Redeemer King. They fully expect crises to erupt each time he preaches, having witnessed them with their own eyes time and again. So a large team of praying people gathers in an adjacent room to pray during the entire worship service. Physically prostrate, they lie on their faces in urgent prayer, pleading for the Spirit to cloak their pastor's preaching with the Spirit's great power. The stories of answered prayer Cymbala tells are inspiring.

Keeping the Feast of Trumpets in practical ways like these tilts a church forward in eager hope for the day when all people will have heard the joyous news that the King has come. When a church lives with that kind of tilt and that kind of power, it really does change its world. Such a church will never become moot, never be irrelevant, and never be ashamed of its answer if its members are asked, "If God reached down

6 Jim Cymbala and Dean Merrill, *Fresh Power* (Grand Rapids, Michigan: Zondervan, 2001), 53ff. Chapter 4, "Spirit Fueled Preaching," is a must-read.

and plucked your congregation out of the city, would anyone but its members notice that it was gone?"

I must speak a word to fellow preachers who are specially called to this ministry. You are under unrighteous pressure today, expected almost singlehandedly to bring success to your ministry, grow the church as if it were a business, and provide creative ministries that are state of the art and in line with best practices. You have to pull all this off while balancing on a tightrope: you must satisfy the demands of the traditional membership, bring change and freshness to reach a rising generation that isn't impressed by tradition, and do this all while remaining debt free. These days, such pressure is not subtle, but explicit. It is also wicked.

The sad result is that many of us who serve in church ministry have taken our eyes off the principal calling of our lives, the calling to trumpet the word of the King. The "watchmen on the walls" are supposed to blow the trumpet as ambassadors of the King to whom they have devoted their lives. But we cannot fulfill such a calling if we are worried about our approval rating or our job. We have but one audience to please. He is an Audience of One.

Already, Not Yet

Earlier I told you about the specific trumpets that would sound in the Feast of Trumpets and suggested how those trumpets shape our understanding of redemptive history. The first trumpet of the feast sounded when Christ poured out his Spirit, sending his church to "preach the gospel to all nations." It commenced the church's missionary calling, her mandate to bring the gospel into a pagan world. Already, the church is playing that horn.

But history is not finished; the day of trumpet sounds is not yet ended. One day the last trumpet will sound. It is the third named blast of the feasts and is referred to in 1 Thessalonians 4:16 and 1 Corinthians 15:52. After that trumpet sounds and Christ returns, there will be no more preaching. It won't be needed.

We live today between those trumpet solos. We still bear the mandate to trumpet the announcement that Jesus Christ is Savior and Lord, for the end has not yet come. Until it does, preaching (both by preachers and by believing truckers and housewives in their own unique way) is "job one" for the church. Whole language groups and cultures have never heard the good news of God. People we know and love have not yet bent the knee to King Jesus.

When men, women, or children hear the sound of the gospel of God and believe it, another trumpet sounds. It is a happy sound, the sound of rejoicing. The great trumpet calls God's people to the next feast, one called *Yom Kippur.* It is a sound—and a celebration—of God's redemption made intensely personal. It is the sound of freedom.

Questions for Further Study and Discussion

1. The chapter explains the ancient custom of "killing the messenger" that brought bad news. How do modern church audiences still "kill the messenger" if they don't like the message?
2. Prayerfully reflect on the preaching you usually hear. Does it point you to Christ? Does it convey the announcement that Christ is Savior and King? Does it righteously meddle in your life, insisting on submission to Christ's lordship? Do you pray before you hear it? Do you answer it afterwards?
3. In what ways, if any, might media preaching (TV, radio, or podcasting, where preacher and audience do not and cannot know one another) affect the message content of what is preached?
4. The chapter suggests that the "incarnational" or "embodied" witness (living open and transparent lives that build gospel-purposed relationships with neighbors) is in fact a powerful form of gospel preaching. How are you playing that trumpet in the Lord's service?

Chapter 7

This Is the Day!

The Day of Atonement

Leviticus 16; 23:26–32

Scott and Jenna were in my office again. Their thirteen-year-old daughter Elizabeth was still cutting herself, this time the razor blade slicing the tender flesh of her lower abdomen. They were, of course, distraught.

I was too, and not just about Elizabeth and the frightening practice of adolescent cutting. Pastorally, a piece was missing from the puzzle. I had known Scott and Jenna for years and had lost track of how many times they had been in my office for one crisis or another. When I broadened my thoughts to include the extended family, I was overwhelmed.

How could it be that one family could consume so much of the limited time and energy our pastoral staff had to offer? Broken marriages, adulteries, repeated adolescent crises that included cutting but also anorexia, all played out over what seemed to be a percussive baseline: frequent cases of depression, despair, and self-loathing that marked the entire family. How could this be in a family headed by parents, now in their sixties, who were, by all accounts, pillars in the church and paradigms of respectability?

In the dark, I did my best to listen, to empathize, to pray. But this particular session was different. This time, desperate for her daughter, Jenna finally began to tell me about her father. She told me things I knew: that he was a powerful man who had amassed a respectable fortune; a generous man who gave freely to his children, grandchildren, and their church; a community leader respected by all. She also told me things that I did not know: that Dad had forcibly committed incest with each of his daughters throughout their adolescence, a period of time stretching nearly twenty years, threatening them—and their mother—with terrible consequences if they failed to keep the family secret.

The notion of "the sins of the fathers being visited upon the children" took on a new twist that day. The tragic impact of one man's sin had shattered dozens of lives over three generations of a family's history. It had warped their view of self, hamstrung their capacity to give or receive love, compromised their ability to trust or respect authority figures. It had robbed them of joy and left their souls bitter and angry. And it had seriously compromised their ability to trust God. They read in their Bibles the words of Jesus: "I will never leave you nor forsake you." But where had he been when Dad destroyed everything that had been pure? Sadly, such a story is altogether too common these days. Statistics suggest that one in four women in North America has been abused by an authority figure in her family. I relate this story here because the ugly reality of sin's comprehensive corruption is not new to this generation. It was, in fact, the theme of the Day of Atonement, the basic truth that would serve to give the Day its meaning.

Cleansing the Defiled

Beginning with the Feast of Trumpets, the flurry of feasts in the seventh month would draw the festal calendar to its completion. Moving from the first to the tenth day of the seventh month brought Israel to Yom Kippur, the Day of Atonement, a celebration so awe-inspiring that it would simply be called "the Day." Over the centuries, it would come to be hailed as the greatest of the High Holy Days, for it brought Israel into the Most Holy Place to meet messianic hope face to face.

YHWH himself issued explicit instructions regarding the complex of traditions that came to define the celebration of the Day of Atonement. The regulations for the feast were introduced with a story that was both extraordinarily brief and most painful. "The Lord spoke to Moses after the death of the two sons of Aaron who died when they approached the Lord" (Leviticus 16:1). We can't be sure what Aaron's priestly sons had done. They may have approached YHWH at an inappropriate time (unrelated to a scheduled morning or evening sacrifice), in an inappropriate way (violating one of the specifications of the offerings prescribed), or in an inappropriate spirit (impure in heart or life). One thing was sure: God's judgment was swift. He is holy, and he insisted that he be so honored by his people, and particularly by those set apart to serve as priests.

Being a priest required a man to have an accurate and healthy sense of identity. Although these were ordinary men, they were set apart for an extraordinary task. Their dress was patterned after and actually made from fabrics that draped the tabernacle. Their world was the building, and the grounds were set apart as "holy unto the Lord." From the garments they wore to the behavior they were expected to maintain, they were, as Tremper Longman III suggests, "part of the tabernacle structure itself."[1]

While on duty, they were to be laser-focused on the Holy One of Israel. The routines of life outside the walls of the tabernacle were not permitted to intrude. Moses reminded his brother Aaron of this—tenderly, most likely, but firmly, too—on the day his two sons died. The extended family would be allowed to mourn the deaths of Nadab and Abihu, but father Aaron and his other sons—priests on duty before the LORD—were forbidden to grieve in any visible way (Leviticus 10:6). How is that possible? "Among those who approach me," God had said, "I will show myself holy; in the sight of all the people I will be honored" (10:3). Remarkably, "Aaron remained silent."

The holiness of God would thus serve as one anchor of the feast known as Yom Kippur. The ceremonies of the Day would soon reveal the other, for they would testify graphically to the extent of Israel's lack of holiness. The Day was, simply, a day that celebrated the cleansing of all that was defiled.

First to be cleansed were the physical instruments of the sacrificial system. These included Aaron and the other priests, stained both with their own sins and by sacrificial engagement with the sins of the people. Aaron needed little reminder of his. His sorry involvement in the golden calf incident stained his reputation and surely pained him deeply, and the sins of his two sons that resulted in YHWH's holy flare-up renewed his understanding of the guilt and pollution of his family.

Aaron was to prepare with a ceremonial water bath and then dress in the sacred garments: linen undergarments covered by a linen tunic,

1 Tremper Longman III, *Immanuel in Our Place*, (Phillipsburg, N.J.: P&R Publishing, 2001), 125.

tied with a linen sash around his waist, and with a linen turban on his head. The turban would bear a gold plate, attached with a blue cord to its front, and inscribed "Holy to the LORD" (Exodus 28:36). When properly clothed, he would enter the sanctuary area with a young bull, later slaughtered "for his own sin offering to make atonement for himself and his household" (Leviticus 16:4–6).

Other tabernacle (and later temple) servants needed cleansing too. Some of these servants were human: the priestly assistant who would lead the scapegoat into the desert needed to be cleansed before he could rejoin the community (v. 26), and the other who burned the hides, flesh, and inward parts of the sin offerings outside the camp had to wash his clothes and bathe himself with water (v. 28). Other servants were architectural: the various rooms and structures within the tabernacle itself, including the Most Holy Place (v. 16), the Tent of Meeting as a whole (v. 16), and the altar (v. 18), would require atonement "to cleanse it and to consecrate it from the uncleanness of the Israelites" (v. 19).

Atonement by Blood

The sad news was that the Israelites' sin had polluted everything. Nothing was beyond its corrupting reach. But there was good news too. It was rehearsed in a ceremony involving two male goats. One was chosen by lot "for YHWH"; the other "for Azazel."[2] The goat "for YHWH" was a sin offering [3] to be slaughtered by the high priest on behalf of the people (Leviticus 16:15–16); the goat "for Azazel" was kept alive, later to be driven out into the desert as a scapegoat.

The differing disposition of the two goats serves to define the rich and variegated notion of *atonement,* a concept that seems foreign and primitive to modern readers of the Bible. Atonement involved blood, lots of blood. While in the Holy Place and shrouded by the cloud of incense, the high priest performed two rituals. In the first, he dipped his finger in a bowl of bull's blood, sacrificed for his sins and those of his family, and sprinkled it on the atonement cover of the ark seven times as *propitiation*, a God-directed sacrifice satisfying the requirements of his holiness.

2 Hartley summarizes the interpretation options for this difficult word: 1. a specific reference to "the goat which goes away"; 2. a more abstract picture of "the goat for removal"; 3. a rocky precipice, the place to which the goat for removal is taken; and 4. a name referring to a demonic being, perhaps even Satan himself. John E. Hartley, *Word Biblical Commentary: Leviticus* (Dallas: Word, Incorporated, 1998). Electronic edition, Logos Library System, S. 237.

3 Longman, pp. 93ff.

Then he would take blood collected from the goat "for YHWH" and repeat the sprinkling ritual as a propitiation for the people.

Sprinkling blood in the Most Holy Place wasn't neat; blood splattered all over. But that was intentional, for the ritual aimed to make atonement for the Most Holy Place because of the uncleanness and rebellion of the Israelites. The pollution of sin had saturated the structure, the space, and the fabric covering the walls, and all needed purging.

God is not bloodthirsty, of course, demanding to be sated by gore. Nor is faith in him a return to the primitive, outdated and irrelevant to sophisticated moderns. To ancient people, and to us as well, the Day sent an ever timely message: sin kills, destroying life on every conceivable level. The message was hard to miss: God wrote it in lifeblood.

It was no surprise then that trembling awe marked the service of all involved in atonement ceremonies. Later in Israel's history, the high priest would enter the Most Holy Place wearing a rope tied around his waist, bells affixed to the fringes of his robe. Should the bells become silent for any length of time, Israel would conclude the priest had died, and his body could be dragged out safely.

Backing out of the Most Holy Place, the high priest repeated the ritual for the broader internal room of the tabernacle; the sins of the Israelites had polluted it as well. He removed still further until he exited the tabernacle structure completely and was standing before the altar in the courtyard. There, the ritual of blood was repeated again, for the altar especially was unclean, stained with the blood of Israel's sins throughout the year (16:18–19).

The Scapegoat

Once he finished the rituals of cleansing within the tabernacle, the high priest would bring out the scapegoat. Placing his hands on the head of the goat, he confessed over it "all the wickedness and rebellion of the Israelites" (16:21). This variation on an ordination ceremony made visible a second nuance of the concept of atonement, namely, that atonement would be accomplished by a substitute. The scapegoat was not killed but was sent live into the desert in the care of a man appointed for the task. It would "carry on itself all their sins to a solitary place" (16:22). A later custom developed that would assure that the goat would not wander back into the community: it was pushed over a cliff.[4]

4 Mitch and Zhava Glaser add the detail that the goat was pushed over *backwards. The Fall Feasts of Israel* (Chicago: Moody Press, 1987), 104.

Hartley suggests that the ancients believed the inaccessible and foreboding wilderness was "the abode of demons or evil spirits." He believes the word *Azazel* is thus a reference to the demonic forces in the world. The scapegoat is not a sacrifice made *to* the prince of demons, but is the banishment of sin *from* the holy people, a sacrifice of *expiation.* It was a *type* of the day when sin will be cast into the fiery depths where it—and the devil—belong.

Whether this translation of "to Azazel" is correct, this much is sure. The "rite of riddance," as Hartley calls it, had the powerful and visible impact of assuring Israel that her guilt had been removed, the atoning sacrifice having taken it away so that its power and lasting effect among the people of God was broken.[5]

The Shadow and the Reality

As we've learned, each of the feasts was a shadow stretching backwards through history, cast by the brilliant redemptive light named Jesus, the Christ. The Day of Atonement is no different. Its components and rituals were visually, emotionally, and spiritually messianic. Each dimension of the rich tapestry of experiences celebrated on the Day anticipated the atonement he would bring. Each taught profound lessons.

The first lesson to be learned was the extent of sin's contamination. Who could fail to be moved by the sad truth that *everything* that served the sacrificial system—from priests to altar, the Holy Place and the Most Holy Place, the implements, walls, and floors—was defiled with the corruption of the sins of God's people?

The second lesson was that God would save by grace—atonement was to be made by a substitute—but grace that was given free nonetheless came at a high cost. There would be blood, and there would be death.

The third lesson was that atonement would demand both *propitiation* to quiet the righteous anger of a holy God, and *expiation* to cleanse the guilt (and, as we shall see, the guilty *consciences*) of an unholy people.

But the lesson that would be perhaps the most profound was one that would wait centuries for an explanation. The New Testament book of Hebrews would provide it. All the ceremonies of Yom Kippur—all the cleansing, all the rituals, all the blood, and all the death—*could not remove a single sin* (Hebrews 10:11). Ultimately, the death of an animal

5 The blood rites in the sanctuary and at the altar cleansed the *pollution* of their sin, while the scapegoat bore the *guilt* of that sin, both together necessary for full expiation of what Hartley helpfully calls the various "trajectories" of sin's deadly reach. Hartley, op. cit., 237.

could not atone for the sins of a people, and a corrupt priest who had to atone for himself could not, finally, atone for others.

Why not? The writer of Hebrews explains, "The gifts and the sacrifices being offered were not able to clear the conscience of the worshiper" (9:9). That is, the sacrifices offered throughout the Day of Atonement could not make a person clean *on the inside*, where the leaven of sin is rooted. A greater priest was needed—and a greater sacrifice. Jesus the Messiah is that greater priest, who "did not enter by means of the blood of goats and calves; but he entered the Most Holy Place once for all by his own blood, having obtained eternal redemption" (9:12). He would offer a greater sacrifice: himself, a sacrifice "unblemished to God," as the many examinations during the week prior to his Passover death had proved. Such a sacrifice will "cleanse our consciences from acts that lead to death" (v. 14).

If the tabernacle and temple priests were part and parcel of the structure, as Tremper Longman III argues, Messiah Jesus was even more so. Recalling the sprinkling of blood on the atonement cover (or slate) of the ark of the covenant, Hartley observes: "On the Day of Atonement it was over this slate that the high priest sprinkled the blood of the purification offerings in order to secure expiation both for himself and for all the people. Now God has put forth Jesus as this Atonement Slate. But whereas the Atonement Slate had been hidden deep inside the Holy Place, Jesus died in full public view. This change in location announces that Jesus' death achieves expiation for everyone who has faith in him."[6]

For the centuries leading to Christ, all the sacrifices on Yom Kippur had been impotent; the Day served only as a type of his better redemption. The sacrifice of Christ was superior: it was offered by a superior priest, and it was offered at a superior place of atonement. Hebrews testifies using a vivid verbal contrast: each Old Testament priest "stands," constantly repeating the same sacrifices over and over, ceremony after ceremony, year after year. But Jesus "sat down" when his offering had been made (Hebrews 10:11–12). The priesthood was no longer on duty. Its work was done with his death.

As if to add an exclamation point, the ancient ritual of the scapegoat driven away from the camp would likewise find its fulfillment in a Messiah whose crucifixion would take place outside the city walls[7] and

6 Ibid., 245.

7 A point Hebrews 13:12 stresses.

along the heavily traveled roads of ancient Palestine, and thus before the eyes of the watching world. For the Day was never meant only for Israel, but as an atoning expiation for the sins of all who believe.

Losing the Meaning

As the long centuries of the Old Testament drew to a close, Israel's eye of faith dimmed, and the shadows of Messiah's atonement became more and more indistinct. The rituals of the Day began to change; slowly at first, but inexorably, they would shift focus and lose their redemptive meaning altogether, despite the overlay and draping of ever more elaborate ceremonies and traditions.

By the time of Annas and Caiaphas, high priests during the years of Jesus' earthly ministry, the more elaborate temple preparations for Yom Kippur began the evening before the Day. The high priest's assistants were tasked to help him get ready, using a process that began with a careful study of the text of the Torah so that he would not inadvertently err in the performance of his duties. Should he become weary of study, they would stand him on the cold marble floor to shock him awake.[8]

On the morning of the feast, he was brought to the place of cleansing, where the ritual bath would take place. Ordinarily, a priest washed his hands and feet before beginning the day's sacrifice. This day, his whole body would be cleansed—five times. At least one of these was in sight of the people, with a linen modesty panel in place.

He would then be garbed in splendor much more glorious than Aaron had been: the white linen of the old days was now trimmed with gold, and the jeweled ephod on his breast and turban on his head also of gold, still bearing the inscription "Holy to the LORD" as prescribed centuries before (Exodus 28:36). The censer he would carry was ordinarily silver; this day it too would be gold.

It was an awesome display. The tension among the other priests would both kindle and reflect the excitement of the congregation: all would be trembling with anticipation as fathers pointed and whispered explanations to their children, who looked on with wide eyes.

The high priest began the rituals, starting with a personal confession of sin over the head of the bull. What a moment: the holiest of holy men confessing his own sins! Then the selection of the goats for YHWH and for Azazel would be made by lot; they would be led away to their

8 In the next few paragraphs, I am indebted to Mitch and Zhava Glaser, op. cit., 91–107.

respective destinies. The priest returned to the bull. With practiced skills, but now clothed with white linen garments, he slit the bull's throat. The priest collected its blood in a basin, obviously a task more difficult than it sounded now that he was garbed in white and nervous to boot. The screams of the beast, the physical effort it would take to control its violent thrashing, and the spurting arterial blood would make the moment unforgettable to every witness.

He was now ready for the heart of the ritual, the dramatic journey into the Most Holy Place. Imagine it with me. The temple of Herod was vast, much larger than the tabernacle had been. The slow walk would take some time, all the while the bells on the fringes of his robe ringing. The priest entered the Holy Place. There, he would perform the requisite rituals with somber gravity. Those accomplished, he could finally approach the heavy curtain that separated the Holy Place from the Most Holy Place, the throne room of YHWH himself. With trembling hands, he parted the curtain to behold . . . ***absolutely nothing!***

For the ark of the covenant, with its gilded atonement cover and cherubim, was gone, carted off to Babylon some six centuries earlier. Nebuchadnezzar had stripped everything valuable from the temple and had taken as pillage all the gold treasures commissioned by Solomon (2 Kings 24:13). All that remained after the exile was a barren platform three finger breadths' high, a foundation stone called *Shetijah* by the rabbis.[9]

Amazingly, the high priest moved methodically through the ritual as if the ritual itself—without the sacrifice upon which it was based and for which it desperately longed—somehow removed the pollution and guilt of sin. He did so because that is exactly what he, and all Israel, believed. After the temple had been sacked, the Jewish religion would have to make a dramatic shift. Their temple had been constructed for worship practices that centered on sacrifice, all oriented toward the ark of the covenant. But the ark of the covenant was gone, and by the time of Jesus, it had not been seen for nearly six hundred years! Without the ark, rabbinic scholars would begin a search for new meaning for the Day of Atonement, a meaning not dependent on blood splashed on YHWH's missing atonement cover. They found the meaning they were looking for in the act of repenting, an act that would not require any sacrifice at all nor temple implements of any kind. Rabbi Akiba (AD 135) would later explain: "The initiative for atonement lies with the sinner.

9 Glaser, 101.

He *cleanses himself* upon the Day of Atonement by way of unflinching self-examination and honest confession, and he resolves not to repeat the transgressions of the previous year."[10] Much later, Maimonides (AD 1204) would be even more blunt, arguing that the act of repenting itself atoned for all iniquity.[11]

In Scripture, repentance had always been important as a sign of a heart broken before the Lord. But repenting does not work magically, the guilt removed just because a person is sorry. I recently watched the televised "statement of remorse" of a convicted killer delivered just prior to his sentencing. With what seemed to be genuine pathos, the young man tearfully apologized to the court, to the parents of the boy whose life he had brutally ended, and to his own family for the shame and embarrassment he had put them through. But perhaps the most pathetic moment came a few minutes later when the judge pronounced a sentence of twenty-five years to life in prison. Stunned, glancing uncomprehendingly from his lawyers to his mom seated behind him, the young man said simply, "But I said I was sorry!"

Through the centuries, Yom Kippur foreshadowed a different message: real guilt abounds in our lives, and it pollutes everything about us. There must be repentance, indeed, but repentance finds its cleansing power not in the fact that we say we're sorry. Rather, the power of repentance is grounded in the removal of sin by the cleansing death of a substitute. Jesus the Messiah was the sacrifice that propitiated the wrath of a just God; he was the scapegoat that expiated the guilt and pollution of the sin of all who believe in him.

Living Clean

One puzzling point still requires some attention; it's the question of redundancy. Why did God even instruct Israel to celebrate the Day of Atonement in the seventh month? He had already foreshadowed atonement earlier in the year in the sacrifice of the Passover lamb, a redemption that seemed complete in itself. At the conclusion of that feast, the priest had cried, "It is finished!"

The answer is related to architecture. Simply put, you don't *live* in a foundation; you live in the building constructed upon the foundation. The foundation is critical, but it is into the living spaces above it that go

10 Joseph Herman Hertz, *The Pentateuch and Haftoras, Leviticus* (London: Oxford University Press, 1936), 162, emphasis added.

11 Cited in Noordzij, *Leviticus* (Grand Rapids: Zondervan Publishing House, 1982), 173.

the furnishings which make life truly *your* life. Your favorite chair goes there, the family portraits hang on that wall, and above the mantle will hang the oil painting you bought that year you traveled to Europe on your twenty-fifth anniversary.

Indeed, the death of the Passover Lamb of God was foundational. It was finished, complete—*sufficient* to cover the sins of all. Scripture speaks with universal overtones: "There is . . . one mediator between God and men, the man Christ Jesus, who gave himself as a ransom for all men" (1 Timothy 2:5–6).

But not all men and women are saved, for not all believe. Scripture is always clear that God demands faith for redemption to be efficient. Faith is not meritorious—you don't earn salvation by your act of believing—but is a gracious gift from God. No one can boast of his faith (Ephesians 2:8-9), yet without it there is no salvation (Acts 4:12).

As we saw in the last chapter, the feast called Trumpets rehearsed the church's glorious task of bringing good news to women and men all over the world. The work of redemption, accomplished in the cross, burial, and empty tomb of Christ, was actuated in the lives of sinners only through the gospel trumpeted by the church.

The Day of Atonement rehearsed what comes next: the amazement and joy of the gospel's personal embrace. It is a simple but astounding truth: if you truly believe, you are truly saved. Paul would say to the Gentile Ephesians: "And you also were included in Christ when you heard the word of truth, the gospel of your salvation. *Having believed*, you were marked in him with a seal . . ." (Ephesians 1:13, emphasis added). To the Corinthian believers he would use words that make you think he was pointedly speaking of Yom Kippur: "Now is the time of God's favor, now is the day of salvation" (2 Corinthians 6:2). This does not merely refer to an opportunity to be seized while available, but one that might soon pass. "Nothing less is intended than that the decisive, long-expected coming of God has dawned, the hour of hours, the day of salvation in the fulfilling, eschatological sense of the word."[12]

I want you to hear this personally: when *you* hear the piercing "trumpet call" of the gospel and bow before your Redeemer-King in faith, that day brings the application of Yom Kippur, the long-expected, long-rehearsed day of atonement, to your life. On that day, the guilt and pollution that have stained *your* entire life are washed away.

12 Herman Ridderbos, *Paul: An Outline of His Theology* (Grand Rapids: William B. Eerdman's Publishing Company), 45.

This is no temporary rinse, repeated weekly in a confessional or annually on a High Holy Day. This cleansing is once and for all. It works within: *your* heart is "sprinkled to cleanse [you] from a guilty conscience." The bath misses nothing: *your* body "washed with pure water" is made pure (Hebrews 10:22). No stain, no blot, no blemish remains.

If you are one who has already trusted in Jesus the Christ, you know the joy such knowledge has already brought to you. I encourage you to rejoice in it daily. Preach it to yourself and to your brothers and sisters in Christ, for Satan the Accuser will try to deceive you into jump-starting a fully cleansed conscience back to guilty activity.

If you are not yet a committed follower of Messiah Jesus, I want you to know and experience the joy that "the Day" can bring to you. I invite you and urge you today to embrace his sacrifice as a substitute for your own guilt, his blood the cleansing for your own filth. I'm not inviting you to engage in a religious ritual, merely mouthing the words of a scripted prayer, merely feeling temporary remorse, merely verbalizing your penance. These do not save apart from a vital and personal faith. "Without faith it is impossible to please God, because anyone who comes to him must believe that he exists and that he rewards those who earnestly seek him" (Hebrews 11:6).

Faith involves seeing things differently, viewing yourself and everything else through God's eyes. In faith, you see much more clearly the ugly reality of the sin that has stained your heart and life. In faith, you repent of it instead of denying it, excusing it, or shifting the blame to other people or circumstances. In faith, you trust the Scriptures that declare that Jesus, the Messiah, is the source of atonement, his blood the cleansing that washes sinners clean, his death the removal of your guilt once and for all.

Not Yet . . .

To trust Jesus the Messiah by faith, whether for the first time in your life or for the first time today, is to celebrate the Day of Atonement and to rejoice in your cleansing from sin.

Keeping the feast involves leaning forward for the fulfillment of God's redemption yet to come. For followers of Messiah Jesus still long for another day when the whole cosmos will be purified of its contamination, and all that sin has broken will be set right once more. Pentecost had empowered and Trumpets had sounded, a gospel harvest begun but not yet complete. So too, the Day of Atonement signals personal redemption yet wants more, much more. For Christ will not rest until he has destroyed all dominion, authority, and power and has "put all his enemies under his feet. The last enemy to be destroyed is death" (1 Corinthians 15:24–26).

Only then will believers—and the whole of creation—finally rest in the presence of God.

Scott and Jenna are still married. I would be lying if I said they lived happily ever after. Each day is a struggle for every member of the family. They sold the homestead after the folks died and don't visit the parental graves very often; going home would be too hard. And, though the memories faded, they never completely left. Still scarred by abuse, Jenna desperately tries to trust Scott, to feel safe in his love, especially in the area of physical intimacy. Both wrestle each day to be open and transparent, to live life in the light instead of keeping secrets to avoid conflict. Elizabeth, their daughter, is making progress; she is now a mother of four. She doesn't cut herself anymore, and her parents' openness and honesty help a lot. Trusting God? They do, but faith's grip is sometimes weak, even slippery, and almost always desperate.

The next feast points Scott and Jenna, and you and me, to a stronger grasp of redemption's healing. In it, we will learn that we can finally go home.

Questions for Further Study and Discussion

1. Walk again through the extensive rituals of Yom Kippur as they are described in Leviticus 16. All of them had a purpose, of course, but several were particularly meaningful in serving to define and model the truth of atonement. Which rituals do you think were most meaningful, and why?
2. What is the fundamental difference between faith and religion?
3. Why isn't the act of repenting sufficient to remove the sins of people, as Rabbi Akiba and Rabbi Maimonides argued?
4. Why, according to Hebrews, is Jesus both a superior priest and a superior sacrifice?
5. The chapter suggests that patterns of sin—sometimes learned from parents, other times developed in response to the sins of others—can mark your life and affect your ability to love and trust God or others. An example is keeping secrets to avoid conflict. Do such patterns mark you? I encourage you today to bring light to the darkness and tell a trusted and believing friend. Most importantly, tell God about it honestly.

Chapter 8

Coming Home

The Feast of Tabernacles

Leviticus 23:33–44; Numbers 29:12–39

Howard Hendricks, longtime professor at Dallas Theological Seminary, was reputed to have advised his students, "Live frugally, but travel often." I've liked that ever since I heard it and have tried to follow his advice.

Some years ago, I was invited to speak for a week to an annual gathering of missionaries serving in West Africa, a part of the world we had never visited before. We were excited. We flew into Banjul, The Gambia, expecting to meet our hosts at the airport. We had to wait a bit longer than usual for our baggage, not a surprising circumstance in international travel. We were relieved when it appeared on the belt, until we noticed one of my wife's favorite blouses hanging from a suitcase that had obviously been opened and hastily, but incompletely, resealed. A more thorough examination of the case revealed jimmied locks, a few minor toiletries taken from my wife's makeup kit, and some missing clothing, including one of a special pair of expensive walking shoes. (One, not the pair. Who steals one shoe?) Such minor losses did not impact our visit very much. Yet the nagging sense of having been violated stayed with us all week.

Compared to the horror stories of many travelers, ours was not a big deal. Yet the uneventful return trip through three separate airports and our arrival back in the States proved to be unexpectedly comforting.

Travelling friends tell of a similar experience: coming home after a long time away is heartwarming.

For the children of Israel, after a long sojourn in a desolate world, the Feast of Tabernacles was like coming home.

The Requirements of the Feast

The last of the *haggim*, or pilgrimage festivals, of the Lord would crown the festal year. Beginning on the fifteenth day of the seventh month, a mere five days after the somber gravity of Yom Kippur, this feast was an exuberant explosion of joy. In many ways, it was unrivaled: none of the other festivals would require as many sacrifices, crowd the narrow roads to Jerusalem with as many pilgrims, or involve as much daily crowd participation as Sukkoth, the Feast of Booths or Tabernacles. Over the centuries, it came simply to be known as The Feast.

As with all the feasts established by God at Sinai and described in Leviticus 23, a complex of requirements would serve to structure the celebration. And as we have seen, practices that developed over the centuries would add new layers to the traditions that marked the week.

Booths

The Feast took its name, Sukkoth, from the temporary booths or tents in which Israel lived during her four decades of wilderness wanderings. Once Israel was in Canaan, after the death of the generation who had journeyed through the desert, God would insist that she "live in booths for seven days . . . so your descendants will know that I had the Israelites live in booths when I brought them up out of Egypt" (Leviticus 23:42–43).

Each family would construct a booth that would evoke memories of desert flora. Palm fronds and the few leafy boughs that could be found near oases—poplar, willow, or myrtle branches mixed with readily available olive branches—were woven together to provide protection from the intense sun and heat of the Middle East, employing a weaving technique used in many applications in the normal course of life.[1]

It was not only Israel who dwelt in booths. YHWH himself had dwelt in one, a portable structure called a *mishkan*, a term that comes to us (via the Latin *tabernacula*) as tabernacle. It too was portable, fabric and leather covering a supporting structure made of poles.[2] Every component

1 The term *Sukkoth* is used elsewhere in passages unrelated to the feast, referring to the structures that could be quickly erected to protect animals (Genesis 33:17), workers (Isaiah 1:8), and warriors (2 Samuel 11:11).

2 S.v. "Mishkah," #5438, in Swanson, *Dictionary of Biblical Languages with Semantic Domains.*

of the tabernacle—from the structural posts, bases and capitals, and animal skins that covered the holy place, to the implements, including altar, sea, candle stands, table of showbread, and the ark of the covenant itself—was made to be carried by the Levites. When God broke camp, he was on the move, and the pillar of cloud by day or fire by night would signal the call for Israel to follow, led by the Levites bearing God's ark. When God made camp, the pillar of cloud or fire would stay put, always visible above his temporary "home," one that marked the seat of his rule.

But the tabernacle and the temple of Solomon constructed after Israel entered the land were types of something even more glorious. Beautiful as they were, they were still only man-made structures that time would erase, structures that could not contain the eternal God who is Lord of all creation. His glory would fill the whole earth (Numbers 14:21). Even Solomon, who built the temple, had to acknowledge its limits: "The heavens, even the highest heaven, cannot contain you. How much less this temple I have built!" (1 Kings 8:27).

Sukkoth was a feast grounded in the temporary structures, but one that always had God's exalted glory in its sights.

Rejoicing

That glory would inspire great joy. Sukkoth was consequently a full-bore party, its booths home base for a wide variety of joyous activities that would stretch out over a full eight days. Framed by two Sabbaths of rest,[3] it was, first, a thanksgiving celebration for God's gracious provision of the harvest. The fifteenth of Tishri would occur around October, "after you have gathered the crops of the land" (Leviticus 23:39), including both the threshed grain and the grapes to be pressed into wine (Deuteronomy 16:13).

The thanksgiving festivities required an extraordinary number of sacrifices, all in multiples of seven.[4] The pattern of daily sacrifices outlined in Numbers 29 included a weekly total of seventy bulls, fourteen rams, and ninety-eight lambs, plus seven male goats as daily

3 Some, like Keil and Delitzsch, think the eighth day, called azaret, was not formally part of Sukkoth, but "the solemn closing of the whole circle of yearly feasts." C.F. Keil and F. Delitzsch, *Biblical Commentary on the Old Testament*, vol. 2 (Grand Rapids: Wm. B. Eerdman's Publishing Company, 1949), 446–7.

4 As we've seen, the number 7 was symbolic of the longed-for completion of redemptive rest. The repition seemed to matter to God; the number 7 dominated Israel's cultic life, not just this feast.

sin offerings; all of these were accompanied by a total of 336 ephahs of flour for meal offerings. These requirements were at least double any of the other feasts, and the number of bulls sacrificed was five times that offered during Passover week.

In one of the few celebrations of the Feast of Tabernacles mentioned in the Old Testament, one that would frame the dedication of the temple of Solomon, the sheer scope of the sacrifices presented to the LORD was astonishing: fellowship offerings numbered 22,000 cattle, 120,000 sheep and goats, and burnt offerings and grain offerings on top of these (1 Kings 8:63–64). The display captured the hearts of the people: they "went home, joyful and glad in heart for all the good things the LORD had done for his servant David and his people Israel" (v. 66).

But Israel's heart soon grew cold. As we've seen throughout this study, her profound spiritual decline under the kings eroded the meaning and distorted the practice of most of the feasts. None was more affected than Sukkoth. It is, after all, impossible to celebrate redemption with a hard heart and a chilled spirit. Over the centuries Israel completely forgot the grace and love that had left divine fingerprints all over her life. The Torah became an afterthought, ultimately consigned to a dusty storeroom within the temple buildings. With its loss, Israel completely neglected the appointed feasts until the reform under Josiah (2 Kings 22). The reforms under Ezra and Nehemiah (Ezra 3:1–4; Nehemiah 8:14–15), especially, would restore Sukkoth to visible prominence and regular observance.

By the first century, Sukkoth still maintained a family orientation, each one constructing and dwelling in its own booth. But the Feast had become a communal affair. Each day the many thousands of pilgrims who had erected their woven booths on every street, alley, courtyard, and flat roof in Jerusalem would join together and lift their exuberant voices corporately to the Lord in a feast the rabbis had come to call *Zeman Simhatenu*, the "season of our joy."

Their expressions of joy involved the use of Scripture. The people memorized, recited, and sang the Hallel Psalms (113–118) in liturgies both family-based and communal. Think of how "Joy to the World" or "Silent Night" shapes your Christmas gatherings, and you get an idea of how these psalms were integral to the Feast. Such songs were more than mere accompaniment; they actually served to *define* the feast in its celebration of redemption. Each psalm praised the God of the covenant for the myriad dimensions of his love and grace, concluding (118:26) in a decidedly forward tilt: "Blessed is he who comes in the name of the LORD."

The children's favorite moment of each day of the Feast of Booths had to be the waving of the *lulavim.* Branches from the palms, willows, and myrtle bushes that had been scrounged in the days leading up to the Feast were bound together and "waved before the Lord" during each day's liturgy in the temple courts. Children took the lead in the physical display; the *lulavim* were shaken so vigorously that the leaves of the branches would fall off. Imagine their enthusiasm! Listen carefully, and you might still hear their squeals of delight.

And, of course, there was food. As always, fruit was essential to a festival, especially the *etrog*, or citron, which was a sweet treat. The day's fare also typically included a wide variety of baked goods and roasted meats. Each day was literally a feast.

Ceremonies within the Feast

Amid the outpourings of joy, a pair of ceremonies unique to the Feast took place on its last day, what John's gospel calls "the greatest day" (John 7:37). These would serve to instruct people young and old about the redemption of which Sukkoth was only a rehearsal, merely type and shadow.

The Drawing of Water

The first of these ceremonies, the drawing of water, would galvanize the crowds: *Nissuch Ha-Mayim* was high drama indeed.

An impressively garbed levitical priest, bearing a golden pitcher, would make the long descent through the winding city streets of Jerusalem from the temple to the Pool of Siloam, accompanied every step of the way by liturgical flutists and a throng of worshipers. No doubt the children raced ahead on the cobbled streets, pressing forward in the enclosed spaces to get a better view. After ceremoniously drawing water from the pool, he would lead the processional back to the temple, entering through the Water Gate. Ram's horns—shofarim—would announce his arrival with a prolonged blast, a quavering blast, and then another prolonged one.[5]

Crossing over the courtyard to stand at the side of the great altar, the priest poured the water into a magnificent silver basin. In a strange twist to the ceremony, the people demanded to see the pouring for themselves, shouting "Raise thy hand! Raise thy hand!" According to Mishnah, this tradition apparently began sometime after 95 BC, when

5 *The Mishnah*, Sukkah 4:8.

one of the Maccabean priest-kings had poured the water on the ground. The people, incensed, had pelted him with fruit. Their indignation was costly; six thousand died in the ensuing massacre.[6]

Although not prescribed in the Torah, the drawing of water had, by the first century, become a central moment in the festivities. The rabbis found grounds in the prophecy of Isaiah 12:3: "With joy you will draw water from the wells of salvation." The Talmud explained, "Why is the name of it called, the drawing out of water? Because of the pouring out of the Holy Spirit, according to what is said: 'With joy shall ye draw water out of the wells of salvation.'"[7]

Jesus kept the Feast as it had come to be celebrated in his day, and that included the ceremony of the drawing of water. In him, in fact, the high drama of the ceremony reached new heights. "On the last and greatest day of the feast," perhaps at the precise moment the high priest dramatically poured the water for all the people to see, Jesus stood and said in a voice that soared above the sounds of the priest and the busy activity of the children: "'If anyone is thirsty, let him come to me and drink. Whoever believes in me, as the Scripture has said, streams of living water will flow from within him.' By this he meant the Spirit, whom those who believed in him were later to receive" (John 7:37).

Isaiah's promise had been extravagant: to a people who once had wandered through a dry and dusty wilderness, their thirst slaked only because they journeyed in the presence of a mighty God who split open a rock to give them a drink, to generations of Middle Eastern people who knew experientially that water meant life, waters *from within* sounded incredible, an impossible dream. Jesus' words offered the key to the puzzle: the long-expected blessing had come, and it had come in Jesus, who would pour out the Spirit to quench the deepest longings of the heart.

The Light of the World

Another ceremony that occurred during the first-century celebration of the Feast was a nighttime event that would conclude the weeklong festivities on their final day with a display so awe-inspiring as to leave the revelers speechless.

Four enormous golden lampstands—seventy-five feet in height—had been set up in the Court of the Women earlier in the day.

6 Edersheim, Alfred, *The Temple* (electronic edition), op. cit.
7 Ibid.

Bowls mounted on top would hold the oil to feed the flames, and young men from priestly families were poised to hoist ten-gallon pitchers up the ladders in order to fill them. The wicks for the oil lamps were thick, twisted together from the linen of the liturgical garments the priests had worn during the previous year. The light from the lamps was bright, and the Mishnah reports, "There was no courtyard in Jerusalem that was not lit up with the light."[8]

The setting for this impressive ceremony was in place; its dramatic meaning could now be revealed. Each person held his breath as the youths laboriously mounted the perilous ladder with the oil and gasped as the flickering flames moved along the soaked wicks to light the night sky. In the awe-inspired silence of the moment, Jesus cried out again, his lone voice rising to declare, "I am the light of the world. Whoever follows me will never walk in darkness, but will have the light of life" (John 8:12).

His claim was both bold and unmistakable. YHWH God, whose glory had once lit up the night sky over their booths and his tabernacle in the wilderness, had returned to his people! For over four hundred years he had been silent; ever since the prophet Malachi had last spoken on his behalf, there had been no word from the Lord. But now God had returned! The "I am" had spoken again. His name was Jesus; he is Messiah!

A Journey Home

It is a challenge for twenty-first-century believers to grasp the full significance of such a festival to an ancient people. Understanding this significance requires more than a sense of the drama of the activities and ceremonies of the Feast of Booths. It also requires an understanding of the meaning of God's booth—first the portable tabernacle and later the majestic dwelling of stone called the temple—in the history of redemption. It has been said that architecture is a language. Many structures in our world were designed to speak, to tell a story, not merely to house as many people as possible with utilitarian efficiency. Many Christian houses of worship, for example, are laid out like a cross, embodying the central message of the gospel. One in which I ministered is a replica of its denominational symbol, a cross intersecting a circle. For centuries, churches were built with soaring vertical elevations designed to exalt God's heavenly majesty by drawing the eye upward. During a more recent period of church architecture, such structures

8 *The Mishnah*, Sukkah 5:2, 5:3.

emphasized the horizontal plane with low ceilings, constructed to accentuate the communal fellowship of the people of God one with another.

God's dwelling place had a story to tell too. Within its architectural layout, the implements and furnishings God designed and positioned would tell the story of the journey of redemption—the return of broken, weary, and restless people to God's sweet rest. The journey from Egypt to Canaan was only the beginning. To "go to temple" meant to take another journey, a journey back to God.

After God brought his people out of Egypt and to himself in the desert, he commissioned Moses to construct his tabernacle. Bezalel and Oholiab, uniquely gifted by the Spirit, would oversee the design and fabrication of the structure and all its components. It was to be the dwelling place of YHWH, the God Who Is (Exodus 25:8); its raw materials had been taken as plunder from Egypt's people and the gods who are not.

The tabernacle was laid out as a rectangle, its outer courtyard measuring 75 x 150 feet, with the long sides on an east-west axis. Within the western half of the courtyard and facing east (Eden), the actual tent housed the Holy Place and the Most Holy Place. In the courtyard outside the tent were placed the bronze altar and the sea. The altar was impressive at 7.5 x 7.5 x 4.5 feet high; the one built later for the temple would be larger at 30 x 30 x 15 feet. A bronze water basin, called the sea, was equally impressive. Inside the entrance of the tent was the first room, called the Holy Place. Within it were located the table of the bread of the Presence, the lamp or candle stand, and the altar of incense. Within the interior room, the Most Holy Place, was positioned the ark of the covenant, the royal seat of Israel's covenant Sovereign.

The layout and orientation of the courtyard and structure embodied the journey. It began outside; the people entered the courtyard through the gate, open and inviting at thirty feet wide. But the warm welcome soon met the chill of reality: worshipers—who were sinful people—entered with a sacrifice in hand because they approached a holy God. The priests received their offering and mediated on their behalf in the slaughter of the sacrifice.

The next stop on the journey was the altar, on which the carcass of the sacrifice was burned; its blood was poured at the base. Then the priest, now bloodied, washed his hands in the sea, a ritual of purification that was required before he could enter the tent. Many regulations governed a priest's entrance into the tent, of course, as the deaths of Aaron's sons Nadab and Abihu had demonstrated (Leviticus 16:1).

After his preparation of blood and water, the priest could now enter the tent. He was enveloped immediately within a cloud of incense. It was dark, the coverings of heavy animal skins and the curtains of heavy woven fabric allowing no light to penetrate. The only light in the room was the flickering illumination of a seven-branched oil lamp. Absorbing most of the light was the curtain, the largest feature within the tent. It was awesome: woven of "blue, purple and scarlet yarn and finely twisted linen" with "cherubim worked into it by a skilled craftsman" (Exodus 36:35). Though beautiful, the angels were foreboding, for they completely blocked entrance into the Most Holy Place.

Cherubim would be even more visible architectural features in Solomon's temple. Beautiful carvings of the angels covered every interior wall, and in the Most Holy Place stood a sculptured pair. Clad in gold, the pair spanned thirty feet wall to wall, the wingtip of one touching that of his on-duty neighbor. And, of course, in both tabernacle and temple, bowing cherubim faced one another, wings meeting, atop the ark of the covenant.

Why cherubim? The common explanation is that angels surround God to sound his praise in his heavenly dwelling place, and the skin-covered tabernacle and the massive stones of the temple were copies of that place (Hebrews 9:23). Indeed, angels do attend the Glorious One. Yet Isaiah 6:2 reveals that the angels surrounding his throne are seraphim, not cherubim. For an explanation of the cherubim woven into the curtain of the tabernacle and later the temple, we must look back to the opening book of the Bible, to the angels stationed to "guard the way" back to God and the tree of life (Genesis 3:22–24).

The Bible opened with a remarkable assertion: "In the beginning God created the heavens and the earth." Note the words carefully: "the heavens" were *created*, as much a part of the world that God made as the earth was. The heavens and the earth were not distinct and separate places, but reflected dimensions of creation. In Eden, "the heavens and earth" were united, and in this one world the God of heaven and the man from the earth dwelt together in joyous harmony. They walked and talked together in the garden in the cool of the day, God deeply invested with delight at what was taking place in the cosmos he had pronounced very good. What conversations God and Adam must have had!

But before God created man and placed him in the garden, a creature named Lucifer, "angel of light," became Satan, accuser and enemy, and led a rebellion against God that began in the heavenlies, among the angelic hosts, and then spread to the earth. When Adam and Eve sinned, the damage was comprehensive. Fault lines snaked across the once-united creation. Earth felt the break—weeds, labor pains, and gender tensions only the beginning of sin's distortion. But the heavens too were affected, both torn from earth—the unity between God and man fractured—*and* ruptured internally. The result resembled an earthquake. When tectonic plates shift or collide abruptly, the incredible forces generated by the movement thousands of feet below ground radiate to the surface of the earth. The power at the surface is terrific—shaping mountains, creating or submerging islands, snapping the greatest constructions of man like so many matchsticks—but the action is much deeper. Similarly, as Paul would say to the Ephesians, the struggle in which the church is engaged is no mere surface battle, but one waged against the "rulers, against the authorities, against the powers of this dark world and against the spiritual forces of evil *in the heavenly realms*" (Ephesians 6:12, emphasis added).

Redemption would be needed not only to remove the sins of flesh-and-blood people on earth's surface but also "to bring all things in heaven and on earth together" again in Christ, thus healing the rupture (Ephesians 1:10). Such a cosmic view of redemption was always on God's radar screen; he always cared deeply about his creation. Jesus made that clear: "For God so loved the [cosmos] that he gave his one and only Son . . ." (John 3:16).

In Genesis 3:22–24, even as the echoes of promised redemption reverberated in Adam's ears, God banished his friend and vice-regent from the Garden of Eden, stationing cherubim to guard the way to the tree of life. He was not worried that Adam would somehow figure out a way to short-circuit the curse and sneak past the angels to steal eternal life by taking a bite from the forbidden fruit. Rather, the banishment was compelled by his love: he would not and could not allow mankind to continue living in Satan's deception, thinking and believing that real life in this world—full and lasting and joyous and meaningful—was possible apart from union with God. Real healing was needed; a band-aid wouldn't do.

Cherubim would be on duty to make that point clear.

It was these cherubim, once posted east of Eden to guard the holiness of God and testify to his redemptive love for man, whose features were woven into the curtain of the tabernacle. Getting past them would require an act of God.

The priests tried, of course; they engaged the journey with seriousness of purpose, fully aware of sin and its cost. They were diligent to offer sacrifices, collect blood, and follow the prescriptions of the Torah. But the sacrifices of bulls and goats wouldn't get it done, even if all the rules were followed; there was always another day, another year, another bull or goat, more blood. The writer of Hebrews would later say, "It is impossible for the blood of bulls and goats to take away sins" (10:4).

No, the journey began at the gate, moved slowly to the altar and the sea, then entered the Holy Place. But there it stopped. There was no getting past the massive twenty-four-foot curtain with its mute but foreboding guardians.

Until God released them from duty.

At the moment of Jesus' death, "The curtain of the temple was torn in two *from top to bottom*" (Matthew 27:51, emphasis added). Simply put, heaven's Lord dismissed the guardians, opening up the way for sinners to come home to God.

Real life with God was possible again. It would be like the life Adam and Eve had once enjoyed with God in the garden, a life where God would be a daily companion, a sweet friend even as he was creation's Lord. It would be a life of fellowship, a life without shame. It would be the kind of life Jesus had called *eternal life*. It would not arrive all at once, but new life would really and truly begin in Jesus the Christ. Notice the verb tenses the apostle John uses: whoever hears and trusts Jesus "*has* eternal life" and "*has crossed over* from death to life" (John 5:24, emphasis added).

What's more, the internal cosmic divorce itself would now be healed, "all things" reconciled to God through Christ, "whether things on earth or things in heaven" (Colossians 1:20). The sinful rupture that had rent heaven and brought enmity to earth had been of cosmic proportions; reconciliation would require healing on a scale no less grand. The story of the death and resurrection of Jesus includes evidence of just such a cosmic impact: powerful earthquakes announced both Messiah's death and his resurrection (Matthew 27:52; 28:2).

Eden Restored

The journey home, from the desolate emptiness of sin into the joyous presence of God, was the hope of Sukkoth. The Feast would not merely reminisce about the "once upon a time, long, long ago" when God had dwelt with Israel and they with him in booths in the desert. It would lean forward; God wanted them to know that a better home was to come.

Once, four rivers had watered the garden. But after Adam and Eve were expelled, they soon learned that water is scarce outside of Eden in the desolate places of life. God would later make special provision—water from a rock (Exodus 17:6)—to awaken his people's hope. Now Messiah gives a permanent supply of living water rising from within, as the prophet—and the festal ceremony—had promised.

Once, every tree was Adam's for food, a bountiful daily buffet. But food was hard to come by outside of Eden; God had to provide manna and quail or Israel would have starved. Now, Messiah offers himself, the bread of life that will sate the deepest hungers of the soul.

Once, Eden had been safe. But outside of Eden life was dark and scary. There were murderers and abusers and rapists and other violent men out there, as the early chapters of Genesis relate. Through the ages, men dwelt in spiritual darkness as frightening as blindness, so thick they could feel it. To show the way, God once lit things up with his presence in a pillar of fire. Now, Jesus declares himself to be the "light of the world."[9]

Jesus came to Bethlehem to bring us home, or perhaps more accurately, to bring home to us. The "Word became flesh and made his dwelling among us. We have seen his glory" (John 1:14). He dwells with us even more intimately in his Spirit. Paul would later declare, using both singular and plural pronouns to make clear he was speaking both to individual believers (1 Corinthians 6:19) and to the community of faith (1 Corinthians 3:16, emphasis added): "*You* yourselves are God's temple"; "God's Spirit lives in *you*."

Already, Not Yet . . .

Neither the structures of the ancient temple nor those of modern churches contain God, of course. Nor does he live in a heaven that is far removed from earth. He dwells among a people from every tongue and from all nations, within a "new Jerusalem" that is not in Palestine. God's address is *on earth* in a city/bride/church that needs no temple—nor a sun or moon for that matter— "for the glory of God gives it light and the Lamb is its lamp," providing sufficient light in the darkness that even the nations can see (Revelation 21:22–24). In the last chapters of the Bible, only the mysterious language of apocalypse will do: collapsing

9 It is intriguing that after the narrative of John 7–8 that was shaped by Sukkoth, the theme of chapter 9 is blindness. Jesus' healing of a blind man by having him wash in the pool of Siloam would contrast markedly with the spiritual blindness of the Pharisees, who refused to live by the Light of the world.

future into present, it describes this glorious dwelling of God, this kingdom of heaven that began with Jesus' appearing and is extending in and through his church.

Although such passages make hopeful eyes twinkle and longing hearts beat faster, reality crashes in; life doesn't look much like heaven yet. This world still has dark pockets, shadowed alleys that awaken cold fear, reminding us of guilt and shame. Some are places, like urban streets filled with drugs, fear, and violence. Some are people, cruel and vicious, who use their power or position to abuse the weak and defenseless. Others are memories, sin's scars buried deep in the recesses of the mind.

The dark pockets of life make living the new life, eternal life, an exercise of faith. It takes different eyes to see God and believe good news amid the ugliness and bad news of a normal day. It takes the new kind of vision called faith to trust him for deep healing when the eyes of the flesh see only the surface damage. The writer of Hebrews would say it simply: "Now faith is being sure of what we hope for and certain of what we do not see" (11:1).

Here, in the gloaming, where life is lived between the dark and the full light of day, we live life in hope: hope for better days, hope for a better world.

Coming home to God had been the hope of Israel's life and worship through the centuries, its journey rehearsed in the tabernacle and temple, its joy tasted in Sukkoth. But the final home of God's people will be richer by far than they—or we—could possibly imagine. Paul told the Corinthian church:

> No eye has seen,
> no ear has heard,
> no mind has conceived
> what God has prepared for those who love him" (1 Corinthians 2:9).

A festival called Jubilee would show just how amazing it will be.

Questions for Further Study and Discussion

1. Read John 7 and 8:12–30. How does knowing the context of the Feast of Tabernacles help you understand the passage? What does "living water" mean for thirsty souls (7:37–38)? Discuss what it means that Jesus is "the light of the world" (John 8:12).
2. Find (on the Internet or in a good study Bible) a diagram of the tabernacle.

   Do a verbal "walk through" of the "journey" the chapter describes. Make sure you understand the function of all the furnishings.
3. Discuss the rending of the temple curtain at Christ's death (Matthew 27:51). Why is it important to note that it was top to bottom?
4. Discuss the chapter's claim that redemption in Christ will affect both "the heavens and the earth." Does this affect the way you think of the future?

Chapter 9

On Earth, as It Is in Heaven

The Year of Jubilee

Leviticus 25:8–55; Luke 4:16–21

A good friend who is a mature follower of Christ recently admitted to me that he struggled to pray "Come quickly, Lord Jesus!"—the desperate prayer and ultimate longing voiced on the Bible's last page. He admitted that praying such a prayer seemed to rub a blister on his sense of daily calling. My friend knows he is saved for a purpose: to live joyously and purposefully for Christ in all that he does. He knows that a life lived for Christ is not in vain but is actually God-pleasing worship, a daily offering of praise to the King. For one with such a robust worldview, praying for Jesus to return seems like praying for a shortcut, an easy way out, an escape from what believers were redeemed to be and to do.

His quandary is not that he does not want to see Jesus face to face and delight in his presence. His admission revealed a common confusion. Many believers today have been led to think that life lived in this world of sin and sadness is only something we do while we are waiting and preparing to move to a new address. Because this world is sinful and full of evil and because our permanent destiny is to be heaven, many Christians think that they should not become deeply engaged in this world's culture, but rather keep it at arm's length to maintain a holy separation. Hymn lyrics confirm the strategy and make it sound acceptable: "This world is not my home, I'm just passing through" is a common refrain.

But such a view is distorted on two levels: it undervalues the purpose and value of life lived for God now, and it portrays an inaccurate view of heaven as our future destination. As God's people began their life together, he gave them a clearer understanding of both the significance of life now and the hope for the future by commissioning a year-long feast called Jubilee. It was a festival that would stitch a golden thread into the warp and woof of daily life, one that would help to weave a tapestry made up of life's diverse cultural activities (economic, judicial, agricultural, relational) and its temporal dimensions (past, present, and future). That golden thread would serve both to decorate and to anchor the tapestry: it would add a hopeful sparkle to the dreary restlessness of sinful days, yet secure life today to its certain future in God's coming kingdom.

The Year of Jubilee is one of the least understood of the festal celebrations established by YHWH in the Old Testament. It was not one of the annual feasts commissioned by the Lord; rather, it was actually one of the Sabbaths whose regulations had provided an overall structure to Israel's life. As such it showed the direction of redemptive history, moving God's people and the whole of creation from restlessness to rest. But if the weekly and annual Sabbaths—and the feasts we've studied in this book—were rehearsals of that rest, Jubilee was to be the final dress rehearsal.

Defining the Term

The Year of Jubilee was to commence with the blowing of the shofar on the Day of Atonement in the fiftieth year, the year after the seventh cycle of Sabbath years. The number seven had long been for Israel an important symbol of the completion of redemption's rest, but the celebration following the seventh cycle of seven years did not traffic in subtlety. Its regulations required the trumpet to sound not just at the temple, but to "proclaim liberty throughout the land to all its inhabitants" (Leviticus 25:10). The words should sound familiar to American readers; they are inscribed on our Liberty Bell.

The word *jubilee* comes from the Hebrew word "to blow the horn" and is rooted in the name Jubal, the father of musical instruments (Genesis 4:21). It was a majestic trumpet concerto: rehearsals would begin with the sound of the shofar on Yom Kippur, then layer a glorious top line—perhaps a piccolo trumpet—on Sukkoth a mere three days later. Jubilee's opus would sound God's soaring reign of grace in the sweet tones of liberty and forgiveness.

The word for *liberty* used in Leviticus 25:10 connotes "free flowing," as water that has overflowed its banks, cresting above them to rush willy-nilly across the arid land. The extent of the liberty Jubilee announced was similarly unrestrained. Sabbath days and years would provide a lovely gift of liberating rest to man and beast, a gift flowing to bless even the land (25:4–5; 11–12). But Jubilee's rest would reach much farther. Each Israelite was called to "return to his own property," a summons that was much more than a folksy opportunity for a family reunion at one's ancestral home, but one that served as the striking announcement that original land grants would be restored. Property sales registered since the original tribal allocation of land under Joshua were to be viewed as leases based on the number of years until the next Jubilee. With its arrival, all leases were up, and the property reverted to the original recipients of God's gift.

This was radical. Land was not only returned to those who had a proven record of being good farmers and managers, but poor farmers, too, those who couldn't grow corn in Iowa in a good year and whose crops were choked by weeds because they had been too lazy to cultivate or irrigate, received their land back as well. And the principle applied to other property too: homes lost for failure to pay the mortgage or sold to satisfy a bad debt were returned to the original owner. Israel would have a long history with the "right of redemption," a custom that would allow Boaz to redeem Naomi's estate by way of a payment. In Jubilee, property would revert to the original owner without payment of any kind (Leviticus 25:28, 31).

Sound crazy—even illogical? Indeed, but that's the risk of true freedom. Once the water crests the banks, it flows with reckless abandon; there are no restrictions or constraints.

Only one factor would shape the freedom Jubilee granted: the heart of God. What enabled Jubilee was his sovereign claim to all the land and property. "The land is mine," he said, "and you are but aliens and my tenants" (Leviticus 25:23). And what fueled Jubilee was the love of God. His love flowed freely, not only to the successful, the achievers, and the winners, but even—and especially—to the poor, the orphan, the widow, and the alien.

In the pagan nations of the ancient world, poor debtors would sell themselves, their slave labor paying the obligation they had incurred. But among the Israelites, debtors would never be permitted to sell themselves as slaves. They could hire themselves out to pay off their debts, but theirs would be work with dignity, not forced servitude.

Those rules were built into the system of laws established under Moses, and they governed Israel's life throughout her history. But Jubilee went further: every Israelite was released from every debt, set free to return to his own clan and the property of his ancestors (Leviticus 25:41).

There were slaves in Israel, of course; they came from the foreigners who either chose to dwell among the Israelites or had been defeated in battle and captured as booty. Even these were released in the Year of Jubilee (25:54). The grace of God that had once set captives free from Egypt would extend to the non-Israelites within her borders.

John R. Schneider argues that Jubilee was not designed as a socialistic redistribution of wealth aimed to equalize the playing field between the poor and the rich. He observes that aliens did not receive property; the restoration of property was for Israelites alone, those to whose families the land had been originally allocated. Aliens from other nations would taste grace but would not receive land. This was neither unfair nor prejudicial but actually extended Jubilee's grace: it would be Israelite property owners who would show future mercies through the gleaning laws and the tithes that would feed Levites and the poor.[1]

Jubilee simply reset the divine economy of grace.

A Forward Tilt

The combination of the perceived illogic of Jubilee and the faithlessness of the people of Israel serve perhaps to explain why this feast of feasts was never celebrated in the land during the Old Testament. Not once did its trumpet ever sound.

This is no surprise for, as I suggested above, such free-flowing grace does not mesh with the ways of this world; grace doesn't cascade from hearts much more at home with the bookkeeping spirit of the flesh. In the flesh, we are much more comfortable rewarding achievement, lauding accomplishments, and punishing laziness or folly. Israel, a people whose covenant life had once begun with unmerited grace, quickly and irrevocably returned to the old ways. Boundless grace was too much for her stony heart.

Because Jubilee was never celebrated in the long centuries of Israel's life, it is no surprise that there is only one other hint of it in the Old Testament, a prophecy made by Isaiah that would lean forward eagerly for Jubilee in the new world Messiah would bring.

1 *The Good of Affluence: Seeking God in a Culture of Wealth* (Grand Rapids: William B. Eerdmans Publishing Co.), p. 83.

The Spirit of the Sovereign LORD is on me,
because the LORD has anointed me
to preach good news to the poor.
He has sent me to bind up the brokenhearted,
to proclaim freedom for the captives
and release from darkness for the prisoners,
to proclaim the year of the LORD's favor
and the day of vengeance of our God,
to comfort all who mourn,
and provide for those who grieve in Zion—
to bestow on them a crown of beauty
instead of ashes,
the oil of gladness
instead of mourning,
and a garment of praise
instead of a spirit of despair.
They will be called oaks of righteousness,
a planting of the LORD
for the display of his splendor (Isaiah 61:1–3).

It was this prophecy from Isaiah that served as the announcement at Jesus' debut party.

Luke's gospel began with Jesus' birth narrative, moving quickly to his baptism and the temptations in the desert. Soon, Jesus commenced his public ministry in Galilee and then returned to Nazareth, the town in which he had been brought up (Luke 4:16). There, on an ordinary Sabbath day, surrounded by family and old friends, he took up the scroll handed to him. It was the Isaiah scroll, and he unrolled it to chapter 61 and read the passage cited above. When he finished reading he sat down.

The ordinary Sabbath synagogue service took an extraordinary turn. As all looked at him, he said simply, "Today this scripture is fulfilled in your hearing (v. 21)."

For a split second they wondered whether their ears were playing tricks on them. They were initially polite, even complimentary, about how well the hometown boy had spoken in public—"and him only a carpenter's son!" They soon turned surly. Jesus pressed his claim further and compared their polite, conservative unbelief to the hard hearts the prophet Elijah had encountered. The surly became murderous. Taking the hometown hero to the cliff of the hill, they intended to make of him a hometown martyr. They knew full well what he was saying—he was claiming to be Messiah—and they wanted to kill him for it.

The story had just begun. The trumpet blast—preaching in the synagogue—had only announced Jubilee's inauguration; Jesus' ministry would now enact it. Leaving Nazareth, he went immediately to the towns and villages surrounding his hometown, releasing the flood of liberty that would characterize the arrival of Jubilee, a reign of grace Luke would call the kingdom of God. In Capernaum, he exercised royal authority to cast out evil spirits that had enslaved many, then healed Peter's mother-in-law and many others. That set off a stampede. Crowds thrilled with the free flow of grace brought everybody they knew who was sick. Jesus healed them all. Even demons got into the act, shouting an unintended gospel even as they were being exorcised: "You are the Son of God!"

Heaven on Earth

The Old Testament Year of Jubilee was not intended to be a vacation, an interruption to the routine commemorated every fifty years to break the dreary loop of life with a sweet surprise. It was to have been a rehearsal of the coming of a new world order, a new regime, a new way of living life that would be simply heavenly.

I mean that literally. The Year of Jubilee that Jesus inaugurated at the inception of his earthly ministry was the planting of the seed of the "kingdom of heaven" into the soil of earth.[2] Heaven's realm would come in under the radar screen, not with fanfare and a mighty army, but like a mustard seed (13:31), as invisible to this world as Jesus was to the first-century Roman Empire. Like wheat, the seed would have to fall to the earth and die (John 12:24) before it could produce fruit. But its firstfruits, waved on resurrection morn, would begin the harvest of the "new heavens and new earth." Its full flowering would await Jesus' return.

As I've suggested throughout this book and especially in the last chapter, Jesus' proclamation of the kingdom of heaven, or eternal life, is a striking contrast to popular contemporary views of heaven. Some of these modern views of heaven are quite secular. In the film *Field of Dreams,* Iowa farmer Ray Kinsella's reincarnated father returns to a cornfield baseball diamond to assure his perplexed son (actor Kevin Costner) that there really is a place called heaven, "the place where dreams come true." A more postmodern perspective is offered in the fictional work of best-selling author Dean Koontz. Character Odd

2 As he would later describe in Matthew 13.

Thomas channels Elvis and other "lingering dead" (ghosts who do not go to their final reward immediately), explaining his view of heaven through his characters:

> Over the years, I have had reason to believe that most of the lingering dead are those who are destined for a better world than this one, if only they will receive it. They resist moving on for a variety of reasons, none of them rational. Elvis had loved his mother so profoundly and lost her so early, that after his death he longed to leave this world and to be in her company once more. But because he felt that he had not lived his life in a manner that she would have approved, because he was loath to face her judgment of his drug use and his promiscuity and his general dissolution, he had lingered here until at last he became convinced that what waited for him was forgiveness that surpassed understanding.[3]

In her best-selling book, Maria Shriver, wife of Arnold Schwarzenegger and niece of John F. Kennedy, explains heaven to children. According to Shriver, heaven is

> a beautiful place where you can sit on soft clouds and talk to other people who are there. At night you can sit next to the stars, which are the brightest of anywhere in the universe . . . If you're good throughout your life, then you get to go to heaven . . . When your life is finished here on earth, God sends angels down to take you up to heaven to be with him.[4]

Contrary to such pop theologies, heaven, according to the Bible, is not merely a spiritual destination, the after-death address of people who qualify. It is instead a realm in which believers in Jesus the Messiah hold their principal citizenship now. In this realm, life is of a different kind, for in it life is not only lived on earth and in time, but derives its impetus and draws its fuel from the heavenly and the eternal. It is thus eternal life (the term John's gospel uses), the life that begins not with physical birth but by spiritual rebirth (John 3:3–5). It is lived by faith, pulses with a new heart, and reflects a prayerful intimacy with God. This kingdom of heaven, this new kind of life, stretches to embrace both present and future, both the spiritual and the physical dimensions of existence.

Understanding what the Bible teaches about heaven requires us to review what many of us have thought happens after physical death. Ask most Christians about that, and they'll tell you, "When you die, you go to heaven." For proof, they cite the story of the thief on the cross. Jesus

---

3 *Odd Hours* (New York: Bantam Books, 2008), 156.

4 *What's Heaven?* (New York: St. Martin's Press, 1999), in N. T. Wright, *Surprised by Hope: Rethinking Heaven, the Resurrection, and the Mission of the Church* (New York: HarperOne, 2008), 17.

told him that he would be with him "today in paradise." True enough. But where is paradise, and, more importantly, is paradise heaven? It would appear that it is not, at least not the heaven many think of when they use the word. At the end of that day, Jesus' body would be in the grave awaiting resurrection, not somewhere up in the skies. Paradise in Scripture certainly isn't Ray Kinsella's ball field, Odd Thomas' s final reward, or Maria Shriver's fluffy future but refers instead to the blessed joy in God's presence enjoyed by those who die in the Lord. Believers whose bodies lie in the grave are embraced now in the Father's love and in Christ's presence; yet they await more. Paradise is not a person's final end, not his ultimate destination; there will be a bodily resurrection, as 1 Corinthians 15:12–34 so clearly teaches. The graves will be opened, the dead in Christ will rise, and they will meet the Lord in the air (1 Thessalonians 4:17).

Then what?

A common assumption is that they will then go away, leaving earth behind. But where will they go? What is their destination? Is heaven located elsewhere? That seems to be the view of many North American Christians seemingly influenced by a series of best-selling novels about the rapture. N. T. Wright's wry summary of such pop theology is worth repeating: "God's people will be caught up literally into mid-air, leaving homes, cars and family behind and escaping forever the space-time world as it goes spinning off to its doom." [5]

The truth is that those who have been raised from their graves and go out to meet him will return with him to a renewed earth, not leave it behind. Paul declares in 1 Thessalonians 4:14 that "God will *bring with Jesus* those who have fallen asleep in him (emphasis added)." These momentous events evoke images of the arrival of a victorious Caesar, feted by the populace along the road as he arrives to thunderous acclaim in a newly conquered city. More importantly, the description of the rapture and return echoes Jesus' first triumphal entry, when the crowd came out from Jerusalem to meet their King, only to return with him to his royal city (Matthew 21:8). This time, it will be clear to all that he is the true and only Lord of heaven and earth and that Caesar's empire—and all modern ones—is "only a parody." [6]

Further, "the heavens," as we saw in the last chapter, is a term almost always paired in Scripture with "the earth" to describe the whole of

5 *Paul in Fresh Perspective* (Minneapolis: Fortress Press, 2005), 55.
6 Ibid., 56.

creation. Such a pairing is based on Genesis 1:1: "In the beginning God created *the heavens and the earth* (emphasis added)." This use of "the heavens" obviously refers to something other than the after-death address of saved people. It suggests instead that dimension of God's creation in which the enmity announced in Genesis 3:15 plays itself out in the realm of angels and demons, fueling the same in the world of people and nations. The cosmic scope of the battle bears repeating: "For our struggle is not against flesh and blood, but against the rulers, against the authorities, against the powers of this dark world and against the spiritual forces of evil *in the heavenly realms*. Therefore, put on the full armor of God" (Ephesians 6:12–13, emphasis added).

When Christ's redemption completes God's purpose, "the heavens and the earth" will be reunited, healing the tear in the fabric of creation that divided what was once united. God will bring all things in heaven and on earth together, reconciling them through the cross of Christ (Colossians 1:16–20). Then reconciled, the children of the second Adam will walk and talk with God as the first Adam had once done in the garden, their joy and delight in his presence taking place on a redeemed earth. The angels of God will not need to wage war for us against their fallen former colleagues, but will praise God with us for the victorious grace of Christ.

This is as it should be; it is for life on earth that God created mankind, placing us here to enjoy him and live for his glory as those who bear his image and reflect his glory. When life is once more as it was supposed to be, heaven and earth will have been joined as one.

> Jake was sixty-five, an old bachelor who had lived on the fringes of life in a small town in the rural Midwest. Mentally challenged, he was sharp enough to recognize—and feel in his soul—the cruel taunts of his neighbors. Over time, he became quiet, even reclusive, finding his satisfaction in his work as a farm laborer, dealing daily with huge Holstein cattle that never mocked him. His only weapon became his extraordinary hand strength. When people made fun of him, he'd offer to shake their hand; they'd do it only once. Jake would squeeze until they cried "uncle" or something would break. Then the taunting would stop—at least the taunting he could hear.
>
> Yet Jake loved Jesus Christ and had a better grasp of the twin realities I've been speaking of than most. On the one hand, he knew—experientially—that here and now life is not as it is supposed to be but bears the undeniable marks of sin and evil. He felt it in the

mockery of his neighbors; he felt it in his own anger. On the other hand, Jake knew his Bible, and so he was eager to taste the glories of the new heaven and the new earth. He used to shout it to his young pastor across the town square. "Mornin' Pastor," he'd holler. "Gonna be fun farming on the new earth. Ain't gonna be no weeds in heaven!"

His neighbors scoffed. Jake was right.

Jubilee People

Jake was a Jubilee man, a citizen of the new creation. People like Jake, believers who know who they are in Christ and have a faith-shaped sense of where life is headed, are spreading heaven's kingdom on earth. For such people, this is the daily way of life in Christ. They live in radical grace, giving life today to the shape of things to come tomorrow.

As observed earlier, N.T. Wright calls such people "citizens of heaven, colonizing the earth." I love that. Their lifestyle is strategic, displaying to the people of the earth what God's heavenly reign of grace looks like—today, and even more so tomorrow. Paul said that the church's unity—one that joins into one body Jew and Gentile, male and female, bond and free—is a mystery that would display the good news to the warring angels and demons, "the rulers and authorities in the heavenly realms" (Ephesians 3:10). Peter echoes this, declaring that believers' "good lives" would mute the mockery of a world that does not understand holiness and so impugns its motives (1 Peter 2:12). This is *mysterion*, mystery, revelation from God that could never be grasped by mere human logic. Here's how mystery works: if the unthinkable can occur, if the irreconcilable actually can be reconciled, if scoundrels can be truly changed by the gospel so that—in the power of the Spirit—they bear the fruit of transformed lives, then heaven truly is breaking in, sin's cosmic rupture is truly healing.

During my lifetime, few places on the globe have tasted the bile of fear or trembled at the horror of violence more than Belfast, Northern Ireland. For decades, sectarian strife has caused death and destruction in its streets. What is particularly sad is that the strife is perpetrated in God's name: Catholic versus Protestant, both claiming to stand on God's side, yet divided so sharply by hatred that reconciliation has been a vain dream.

Until, that is, the new world breaks into the old.

Charles Colson tells a story of reconciliation that took place against the background of such violence and hatred. It is a story of Liam, a

Roman Catholic, and Jimmy, a Protestant.

> Liam had been the last member of the famous Maze Prison hunger strikes . . . in which Bobby Sands led nearly a dozen fellow terrorists to their deaths. When Liam's turn came, he starved himself for 55 days. Blind, weak, and near death, he was visited by his mother, who convinced him to break the fast. During Liam's recovery, he realized he had to make a choice between his cause—the Irish Republican Army—and Jesus Christ. He chose Christ—and from that point on, his faith led him to radical steps of forgiveness and love. He began eating with former enemies, breaking the strict segregation between Catholics and Protestants in his prison mess hall. And eventually, through Liam's witness, Jimmy, a Protestant ex-terrorist, came to know Christ . . . [T]he two stood on a stage before a huge crowd of both Catholics and Protestants. As Liam put his arm around Jimmy's shoulders, he evidenced the power of the Christ who reconciles: "Before, if I had seen Jimmy on the street," he said, "I would have shot him. Now he's my brother in Christ. I would die for him!"[7]

Corrie ten Boom tells a similar story of reconciliation based on her experience in the Nazi concentration camp in which she and her family were imprisoned for giving aid to Jews in the Netherlands during World War II. Her father and sister died in Ravensbruck, and Corrie herself suffered greatly in the camp.

> It was at a church service in Munich that I saw him, the former S.S. man who had stood guard at the shower room door in the processing center . . . He came up to me as the church was emptying, beaming and bowing. "How grateful I am for your message, Fräulein," he said. "To think that, as you say, he has washed my sins away!"
>
> His hand was thrust out to shake mine. And I, who had preached so often to the people in Bloemendall the need to forgive, kept my hand at my side.
>
> Even as the angry, vengeful thoughts boiled through me, I saw the sin of them. Jesus Christ had died for this man; was I going to ask for more? Lord Jesus, I prayed, forgive me and help me to forgive him.

7 *The Role of the Church in Society: Responding to a Watching World* (Wheaton: Victor Books, 1986), 22–23.

I tried to smile, I struggled to raise my hand. I could not. I felt nothing, not the slightest spark of warmth or charity. And so again I breathed a silent prayer. Jesus, I cannot forgive him. Give me Your forgiveness.

As I took his hand the most incredible thing happened. From my shoulder along my arm and through my hand a current seemed to pass from me to him, while into my heart sprang a love for this stranger that almost overwhelmed me.

So I discovered that it is not on our forgiveness any more than on our goodness that the world's healing hinges, but on him. When he tells us to love our enemies, he gives, along with the command, the love itself.[8]

Let me tell one more story, this one set in the context of racism behind prison walls. For over a year, some believers and I ministered to inmates through a weekly Bible study in a state prison facility in central Texas. Month after month, the men sat in self-appointed segregation in the cavernous room: blacks on the speaker's left, whites on his right, and Hispanics (the least of the least in this prison) crowded together in the rear of the room. After one particular session that explained and celebrated the victorious power of the cross of Jesus Christ, over one hundred men stood. Slowly, hesitantly, they turned to face each other. The guards overseeing the room became nervous; more than one put a hand on his riot stick while their captain reached for his radio. Frank eye contact between the races in prison is usually a precursor to violence; this time, it was something else. Heaven was breaking into that fenced-in piece of earth. The men embraced each other in tears and with joy. They had become one in Christ, love, forgiveness, and grace bringing new life to the ugly world topped with razor wire.

There are many ways God's new people serve as the presence of Jubilee, citizens of the kingdom of heaven that is even now flowing freely throughout the world and reconciling all things in Jesus Christ. I'll tell you a few; you may think of many others.

Jubilee people reveal different priorities. They are earth keepers rather than earth abusers. Josh is just such a young man. He's working to earn a doctorate in environmental engineering at a major university. With such a degree in hand, he would be set up for financial success in this world. But Josh has tasted grace in Jesus Christ, and because of it, he cares less about wealth and what it can buy than he does about

8 *The Hiding Place* (New York: Bantam Books, 1974), 238.

glorifying God as a steward of creation. Jesus had once said that God so loved his cosmos that he sent his only begotten Son to redeem it (John 3:16). Josh does too, so he plans to use his degree for redemptive purposes. He wants to develop ways to supply fresh water to people living in parched regions of Uganda, sustaining their physical lives yet hoping to bring them the Living Water of the Feast of Booths, a Messiah who will satisfy the deepest needs of their heart.

Jubilee people are honest, not spinning the truth with cunning and craftiness to serve their own agenda, but "truthing in love," a literal translation of Ephesians 4:15. They bear the truth because they are anchored to Jesus, having broken with the father of lies. Robbie had been a pornography addict for years. His sin exposed, his marriage to Lily was, to use Robbie's words, "on the rocks because she doesn't understand me." The real problem was that Robbie did not understand himself, neither his internal depravity nor the impact of his "no-fault habit" on Lily's heart. Amazingly, Lily stayed the course. She prayed for her husband's deliverance even when she despaired that she would ever see trust restored. Lily could believe he was truly repentant only after she saw that he was truly honest—about everything. She saw the first trickle of Jubilee freedom when Robbie stopped using euphemisms for his sins and began to confess them honestly to God, to her, and to others instead of living behind a façade. The trickle became a stream when he came to understand that God had redeemed him from sin for ministry, one in which he would have to share the shame of his own story in order to help others caught up in similar sins. The flow of grace in Robbie's life began to soothe her broken heart and allowed her to trust him again. The river that comforted and healed them in their troubles now runs like a torrent, flowing from their marriage to bring healing waters to others. Such is the dynamic of heaven: the broken, once healed by God, become his fingers of grace in the lives of those still troubled (2 Corinthians 1:3).[9] Robbie and Lily now anchor a marriage ministry in their church, one that has launched dozens of similar Jubilee stories.

Jubilee people are powerful, more so than they appear in the flesh, for they are filled with the Spirit of God. They possess both courage and self-discipline that the flesh cannot understand or emulate (2 Timothy

9 All references to *comfort* in this section of 2 Corinthians 1 translate the Greek word *paraklete,* Jesus' name for the Holy Spirit. The ministry of believers to one another is an embodiment of the Spirit of God, who is himself the downpayment of the new creation (Ephesians 1:14).

1:7; Hebrews 11:32–38). The tiny old Chinese woman thought she was alone, the only follower of Jesus left after Mao's Cultural Revolution had declared the Christian faith eradicated. The purge had been as thorough as it had been cruel. Mao's wife had declared in the early 1970s that the only Bibles left in China were in museums. Yet Christian missionaries, crossing into the mainland from Hong Kong and desperate to discover what had happened in the silent years since all the earlier missionaries had been expelled, found this lonely soul. She told a horrible story: she had been publicly humiliated for her faith, forced to wear a dunce cap during her trial in the main soccer arena in front of the entire assembled town. As punishment for believing in Jesus, she was given a life sentence: for the rest of her days, she would be required to maintain the open trench that moved raw sewage through the streets of her village. Though ostracized from polite society, she clung to her Savior. When she met the Christian missionaries visiting from the West, she asked simply, "Are there any Christians left in China?" She was thrilled with their answer.

Her visitors returned to their hotel committed to help in whatever way they could. Tearing apart the six Bibles they had taken into China, they took portions of each so as to fabricate—with a hotel sewing kit—one complete Bible out of the many sections, a Bible protected by a cover hastily formed with a piece of fabric torn from a dress. They would leave her the Word of God and still be able to leave the country past a scrupulous customs officer who had warned them sternly that he would personally make sure they left with all six Bibles they had when they entered.

Returning to China some years later, the missionaries visited the old lady again. When they offered her a new Bible, she humbly declined, embracing her old rag-covered one and insisting they give the new one to "someone who needed it." When they inquired if she needed anything else, she smiled and said no. Declining their offers of money and food, she explained: "God is so good to me. He brings me food and money and many other gifts; they float to me in my sewer. I have more than all my neighbors."[10]

Jubilee people are passionate; they "hate what is evil" and "cling to what is good" (Romans 12:9). Their zeal for holy living arises from their knowledge that in Christ they are already sanctified by grace. Grateful for their new life, they want to live it for him more and more.

10 Thanks to John Bechtel for telling me the story and to his wife for her sewing skills.

Bold in their witness (Acts 1:8; 7:54–60; 8:4), they announce the gospel to all people and unashamedly claim all of life for Christ. They do so because God is sovereign, and they revel to be sons who bear his name and live for his glory. They are confident—fearless, in fact—because they are privy to a secret: "The God of peace will soon crush Satan under your feet" (Romans 16:20). The 2007 movie *Amazing Grace* tells the courageous tale of William Wilberforce. A physically frail man who struggled for years with gastrointestinal ailments that laid him low, Wilberforce sparked the movement that broke the back of the slave trade in Great Britain. Though all were against him, from crown to Parliament, from business leaders to churchmen, he was empowered by the Spirit from heaven, and so persevered. The nation, and ultimately, Western civilization, was transformed. Parliament voted to abolish the slave trade in 1807, some fifty-six years before Lincoln signed the Emancipation Proclamation.

Jubilee people may be in the world, but they are not of it. They are citizens of heaven, and from that realm flows the fuel that powers their life force. Though they live in the flesh and experience its sin and brokenness, they are not of the flesh. They taste the good gifts of a new world breaking in, yet are not satisfied. A mere taste is not enough; Jubilee people are impatient for the whole feast. God's Word has them on the edge of their seats; they yearn for heaven's full unveiling. Expectantly, even stubbornly, they lean forward the way the roster in Hebrews 11 did, longing for "a better country—a heavenly one" (v. 16). That heavenly country, its first appearing a mere mustard seed in Bethlehem in Judea, will be revealed fully at Jesus' return.

The dramatic conclusion of God's long redemption story, of which all the feasts were rehearsals and types, is described in its final and most glorious form in the Bible's final chapter. It portrays a heavenly future so beautiful it makes your heart ache. Yet it is a heavenly future that has already begun. Present-tense verbs shift seamlessly into future-tense verbs as the *already* and the *not yet* of redemption intersect. Here the river flowing from the throne of God has already crested its banks and is running freely. The "tree of life," once barred from man's reach by angel guardians, is in play again; bearing a new crop of the fruit (of the Spirit) each month, its leaves are already bringing healing to the nations of the earth. The ancient curse has been overturned, and because it has, God's people see his face again—a bit hazy now, but clearer each day. God's people serve him, but not *in* a temple made of stones and gold leaf; they *are* the temple of the Spirit. Because the curtain has already been torn open, they already enjoy an intimacy with him that makes the old booths look like a cheap pup tent.

The picture at the end of the Bible story is of a new heaven and a new earth that finally reveal what the first was designed to be, but for the rift sin caused. The new creation is a reconciled world in which God is again both beloved Friend and creation's Lord. Once more men and women will reign as Adam and Eve did, exercising dominion over everything to bring glory to the God they worship with every breath. Once more God's people will walk and talk with him in the garden in the cool of the day, no shame of sin causing them to shrink back in fear.

When that day comes, when Jubilee's celebration has touched every person and all of life with freedom and grace, then every knee will bow before the Lord, the rocks will shout their praise, and the trees of the field will clap their hands in joy.

For then, at last, all will be at rest.

Questions for Further Study and Discussion

1. Review Leviticus 25 and the prescriptions for the Year of Jubilee. Can you understand why Jubilee was not ever celebrated in the Old Testament? What do you think a radical display of grace would look like in today's world?
2. Discuss popular understandings of heaven. Compare them with the portrayal of heaven in the chapter. What difference do the two portrayals make to daily living?
3. Is Jubilee a feast that Christians already celebrate, not yet celebrate, or both?
4. Do you personally pray, "Come quickly, Lord Jesus"? What do you mean when you pray it?
5. Do you personally pray, "Thy kingdom come, thy will be done, *on earth as it is in heaven*"? What do you mean when you pray that?

Note to the Reader

The publisher invites you to respond to us about this book by writing Reformed Fellowship, Inc., 3500 Danube Dr. SE, Grandville, MI 49418, USA. You may also email us at president@reformedfellowship.net

Founded in 1951, Reformed Fellowship, Inc., is a religious and strictly non-profit organization composed of a group of Christian believers who hold to the biblical Reformed faith. Our purpose is to advocate and propagate this faith, to nurture those who seek to live in obedience to it, to give sharpened expression to it, to stimulate the doctrinal sensitivities of those who profess it, to promote the spiritual welfare and purity of the Reformed churches, and to encourage Christian action.

Members of Reformed Fellowship express their adherence to the Calvinistic creeds as formulated in the Belgic Confession, the Heidelberg Catechism, the Canons of Dort, and the Westminster Confession and Catechisms.

To fulfill our mission, we publish a bi-monthly journal, *The Outlook,* and we publish books and Bible study guides. Our website is *www.reformedfellowship.net*